MW01485291

The *Mattel* *Archive*

RIZZOLI
NEW YORK

New York · Paris · London · Milan

Timeless Play

It all began in a Southern California garage in 1945—a remarkable collaboration between founders Ruth and Elliot Handler and Harold "Matt" Matson. Designers and engineers, their collective focus on creativity forever changed the way children play. In the process, they created what would become a leading global toy and family entertainment company and owner of one of the most iconic brand portfolios in the world.

They created Mattel.

The year 2025 marks our 80th anniversary. In the eight decades since our humble beginnings, Mattel has thrived by staying true to our mission to create innovative products and experiences that inspire fans, entertain audiences, and develop children through play; and to our purpose to empower generations to explore the wonder of childhood and reach their full potential.

At Mattel, play is our language. In fact, over the years we have evolved our approach to think of the people who buy our products as more than consumers; they are fans, with an emotional connection to our brands. We speak authentically to our fans by reflecting the world as they see and imagine it. We believe this is why our brands are cherished, generation after generation, all around the world.

From Barbie's groundbreaking debut in 1959, the brand has inspired six decades of girls to achieve their limitless potential. Since 1968, Hot Wheels has been igniting the challenger spirit in every kid. Fisher-Price, American Girl, Masters of the Universe, Matchbox, Thomas & Friends, UNO. This treasure trove of brands and many more has made an indelible mark on children's and families' lives and on our culture.

We hope you enjoy this special reflection on 80 years of Mattel. However, more than a walk down memory lane of moments in our heritage, the pages of this commemorative book are meant to celebrate something greater: the wonder of childhood and all its indelible memories, as empowered through the innovation of eight decades of talented designers and creators at Mattel. It is in this spirit that we not only look back; we look forward, because for all of us at Mattel, we believe we are just getting started.

—YNON KREIZ, Chairman and CEO, Mattel

FOLLOWING PAGES, LEFT: Harold "Matt" Matson, Los Angeles, c. 1946.
FOLLOWING PAGES, RIGHT: Elliot and Ruth Handler playing with Hot Wheels Sizzlers, c. 1970.

"*Music. Color.* Action."

CHAPTER ONE

The Innovators

Childhood: a time of growth, learning, and becoming. Most of that process happens through play, the magic that lets children try on different careers, dream of various futures, learn about their own emotions, and develop empathy. While play has always existed, it becomes more when combined with thoughtful, imaginative, even revolutionary toys that speak to children where they are.

Enter Ruth and Elliot Handler, a young couple based in Los Angeles who, in the 1940s, began to foster a dream that would one day become a massively successful—and influential—global reality.

1945–1958

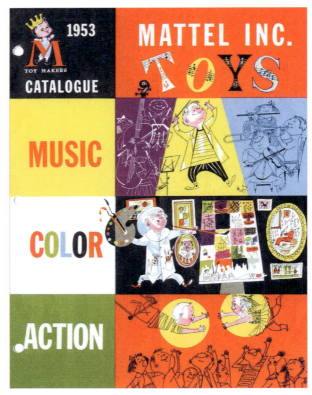

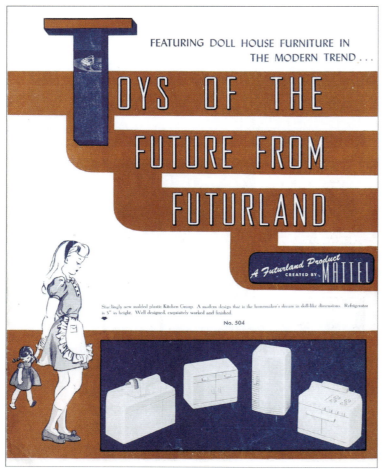

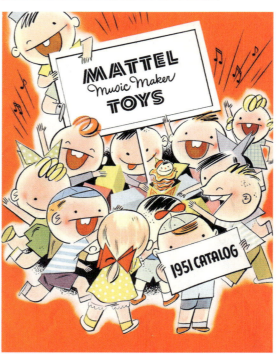

In 1945, frustrated by the lack of control in Elliot and his friend Harold "Matt" Matson's Lucite design work, the Handlers and Matt decided to form their own company. They combined their names, "Matt" and "Elliot," and called it Mattel Creations. A large order of picture frames gave them the capital they needed to dive into what they really wanted to make: toys.

Both the U.S. economy and family life were flourishing with the end of World War II, and Elliot and Ruth saw the need for fresh, fun toys for all of the growing families settling into the suburbs. The Handlers felt strongly that every child should have access to high-quality toys at prices that were affordable for the average American. Most of their toys retailed for under $5 throughout the 1940s and 1950s. In 1948, Matt wanted to retire, and the Handlers bought him out, leaving them as the sole owners of Mattel.

The Handlers recognized early on that it was important to design toys that could be updated year after year, keeping the sales track strong; or to design a mechanism that could be used in a variety of different types of toys, allowing new designs to be created faster. They invested in the concept of a repetitive mechanism, and their unique line of thinking worked: Mattel's first breakthrough was in 1947 with the Uke-A-Doodle, a plastic molded ukulele with a windup music box inside that was then utilized in multiple toys, including the Jack-in-the-Music Box in 1951 and the Hickory Dickory Musical Clock in 1952.

The addition of sound to children's toys was so fresh and inventive that it put Mattel on the map; but the Handlers were thinking even bigger and, in 1955, Mattel innovated once again. Disney had asked Mattel to create branded toys for their new television show for kids, the Mickey Mouse Club. To start, Mattel took the design of the Uke-A-Doodle with its musical mechanism and turned it into the Mickey Mouse Club Guitar. Disney also asked if Mattel would sponsor a segment on the show, which would maximize marketing opportunities for the toy, and for the company at large. At the time, toy companies didn't market on television, and they certainly didn't sponsor TV shows, but Ruth and Elliot saw the potential.

They used every dollar of capital they had to close the half-a-million-dollar deal, and it paid out in huge dividends. The Mickey Mouse Club debuted on October 3, 1955; by Thanksgiving, Mattel was inundated with orders for the Mickey Mouse Club toys and the Burp Gun that they could barely keep up with. They realized that they needed more communication between marketing, sales, and the factories. Ruth developed a system to help predict and track sales, including weekly reports, and created a "retail detail" team that travelled the county, doing product checks and setting up Mattel displays in stores. The company's sales tripled within three years and they continued to scale operations accordingly, opening the door for bigger and even better things.

OPPOSITE, CLOCKWISE FROM UPPER LEFT: Mattel catalog covers from 1952, 1953, 1958, 1951, and 1946. The "Toys of the Future" catalog is regarded as the first official Mattel sales catalog.

Catalog Archive

a MATTEL *Music Maker Toy*

Uke-a-doodle **MUSIC BOX**

TWO toys
in one

TURN HANDLE AND IT PLAYS REAL MUSIC

POP GOES THE WEASEL

LONDON BRIDGE

WHERE, OH WHERE, HAS MY
LITTLE DOG GONE?

A real Hawaiian miniature
ukelele with music box . . .
made of a durable molded plastic, it comes in assorted colors . . .
colorfully packaged . . . priced low for
volume turnover.

Write for prices and information

NEW! . . . The
first successful American
developed toy music box
. . . a sensational new type
musical movement.

No. 418 Songs: Pop Goes the Weasel; Where, Oh Where, Has My Little Dog Gone?

Packed 3 dozen to a carton, shipping weight 18 lbs. Terms: 2% 10 days, E.O.M.
. O. B. Culver City. Regular trade Discounts. Newspaper mats available.

PATENT PENDING

Futurland Toys

Mattel Creations 8436 WARNER DRIVE, CULVER CITY, CALIFORNIA

ABOVE: Sell sheet for the Uke-a-Doodle Music Box, 1949.
FOLLOWING PAGES: Interior pages from the "Toys of the Future from Futurland" catalog, 1946.

FUTURLAND MINIATURES IN SPARKLIN

Excite the imagination of both Mother ar

No. 501
🔺 A Living Room Set that is luxury in miniature. Chartreuse with red trim catches and holds the parents' as well as the children's eye when this set is displayed. Length of the Divan is 4½".

No. 503

🔺 Sheer loveliness describes this tiny piano and matching bench. Colors may be ordered in rose, green or breath-taking crystal. Approximately 3" long by 2⅜" wide. Individually boxed.

Bedroom Set. Sparkling plastic highlighted ▶ with orchid tint is the perfect complement to the rich green spread. Real glass mirror on the dresser. Mattress measures 2¾" x 4". Table lamps are solid. Fluted edged picture adds beauty to this group.

No. 502

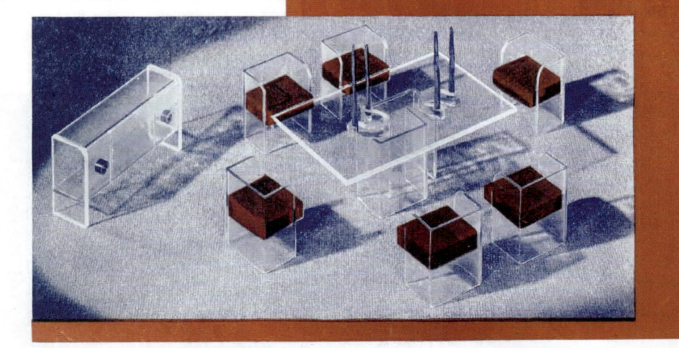

No. 500

◀ Dining Room Set. measures 2½" x 4". designed and achieve note so desired by th today. Clever candl plastic, fitted with imit add to this set's attract

A Futurland Product CREATED BY MATTEL, 5908 S. Main St., Los Angeles, Califor

PLASTICS...

Daughter with dreams

of Furnishings of the

Future.

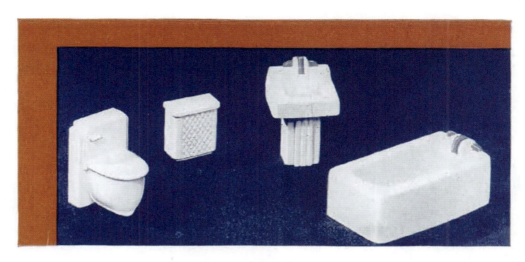

No. 505

◆ Bathroom Set of molded plastic in pastel shades. New design that will attract crowds when displayed. Wash stand is 2¼" in height. Set is complete with bathtub, sink, clothes hamper, and toilet.

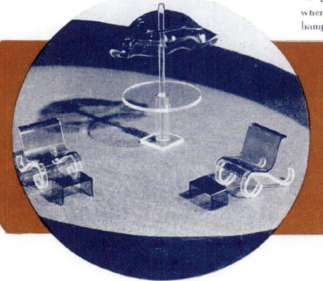

No. 506

◆ Patio Set that reflects the Casual California design. Ruby red and green color combination. Umbrella is removable. So comfortable looking that it invites a siesta despite its size. Umbrella stands 5" from base to tip.

No. 508

◆ Breakfast Room Set. Smart and cozy, complete with four chairs, corner cabinet, clock and fruit bowl. Set is finished in red and blue to delight future wives' hearts.

No. 507

◆ Playground Set. A diminutive playground that will fit in a cigar box. Creates comment and sales wherever shown. Red and green colors put desire sparkle in children's eyes. Height of swing is 4¼".

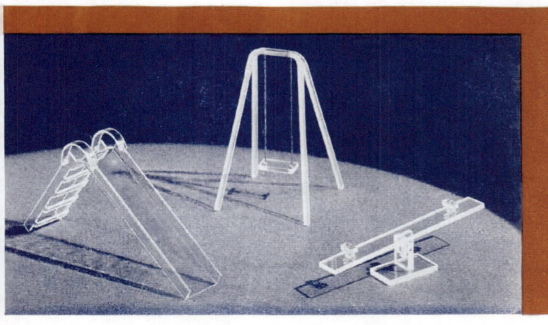

Futurland Product CREATED BY MATTEL, 5908 S. Main St., Los Angeles, California

A new low price for volume sales
Birdy Bank

Colorful:

Animated:

Boxed:

Low Cost:

Youngsters Delight…sturdy animated toy bank. Made of colorful molded plastic in assorted bright colors. Birdy's beak drops coin down the chimney when his tail is tilted…then returns to an upright position… constructed with a simple locking plug at base of bank for removal—Bank on Birdy Bank for toy sales.

No. 406 packed 3 dozen carton, shipping weight 10 lbs. 6 dozen carton, shipping weight, 18 lbs. Terms: 2% 10 days, net 30 days. F. O. B. Los Angeles. Regular trade discounts. Newspaper mats available.

Write for new prices and information

Representatives

Jalof & Lewis
1110 Wilshire Boulevard
Los Angeles 14, Calif.

Toy Market
1424 Merchandise Mart
Chicago 54, Illinois

A. J. Frank
200 - 5th Avenue
New York 10, New York

Russell D. Jesse Co.
511 Spring St., N. W.
Atlanta 3, Georgia

Mattel Creations 8434-36 Warner Drive, Culver City, California

A MATTEL Music Maker Toy

Make their eyes stop, look, and glisten...

RUBE Rhythm Rabbit

A gay wacky dancing rabbit for the Western Barn Dance craze

Patent Pending

Another Mattel Profitunity!

With funny arms and legs that actually move, Rube dances all day long, keeping time to complete musical selections. Fuzzy fabric ears, hands, feet, plastic body. Priced for action, too.

Size 6¼" x 5½" x 5¾"
Red and blue stage.
Display box.

No. 427. Packed 2 doz. to carton. Shipping wt. 21 lbs. Terms: 2% 10 days E.O.M. F.O.B. Culver City. Regular trade discounts . . . Newspaper mats and electros available.

Representatives:
Jalof & Lewis . . . . 1110 Wilshire Blvd., Los Angeles 14, Calif.
Toy Market . . . . 1424 Merchandise Mart, Chicago 54, Illinois
A. J. Frank . . . . 200 Fifth Avenue, New York 10, New York
Russell D. Jesse Co. . . . . 644 Blvd., N. E., Atlanta 5, Georgia

"Mattel has the Secret"

Mattel Creations

8436 WARNER DRIVE,
CULVER CITY, CALIFORNIA

OPPOSITE: Sell sheet for the Birdy Bank, 1948.
ABOVE: Sell sheet for the Rube Rhythm Rabbit Music Box, 1950.

ABOVE: Sell sheet for the Musical Peek-a-Boo Easter Egg, 1950.
OPPOSITE: Sell sheet for the Mattel Movie Show viewer, 1951, a manually operated viewer that showed loops of 8mm film.

Mattel Movie Show

POWERED WITH SPRING MOTOR

LOW-PRICED FOR VOLUME SALES

A "reel" educational action toy with spring-activated die-cast motor. Sturdy red molded plastic construction, with same non-clicking action and shutter as big movie projectors. "Day-light" eye-piece viewer, thumb-lever, gear and flywheel, make for simple operation. 1 loop of 8 mm. film.

Patent Pending

Complete with one loop 8 mm. film.

Size: 2½ x 2⅜ x 2⅝

Mattel CARTOON MOVIE SHOW

No. 429 C—With exclusive new cartoon films by Mattel. Bright, fun-filled action comics!

USES STANDARD 8 mm. FILM

Mattel WESTERN MOVIE SHOW

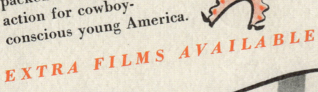

No. 429 W—Real Western thriller movie, packed with plenty of action for cowboy-conscious young America.

EXTRA FILMS AVAILABLE

"Mattel has the Secret"

Representatives:

Jalof & Lewis . . . 1110 Wilshire Blvd., Los Angeles 14, Calif.
Toy Market . . . 1424 Merchandise Mart, Chicago 54, Illinois
A. J. Frank . . . 200 Fifth Avenue, New York 10, New York
Russell D. Jesse Co. . . . 644 Blvd., N. E., Atlanta 5, Georgia

. . . Packed 3 dozen to a carton. Shipping weight 14 lbs. per carton. Terms: 2% 10 days E. O. M., F. O. B. Culver City. Regular trade discounts. Newspaper mats and electros available.

Mattel Creations

8436 Warner Drive • Culver City, California

Chromatically tuned with real jet black keys that actually play

Futurland GRAND

Futurland GRAND

Dimensions
Width: 8½ inches
Length: 11½ inches
Height Overall: 7¼ inches

Attractions:

★ 17 Plastic keys
★ Real sharps and flats
★ Chromatically tuned
★ New type, patented Sound Board
★ Feather touch action
★ Colorful two-tone variegated plastic
★ Removable legs and music stand
★ Colorfully packaged
★ Complete with music

An all-year musical toy favorite... the musical toy with 17 plastic keys, 10 white and 7 jet black keys that actually play... the only table model toy piano that has sharps and flats. Fabricated of sturdy washable molded plastic in bright toy-tested colors... Futurland toys have always been leaders in sales, profits and consumer acceptance. Amazingly low priced for volume turnover.

Write for prices and information

No. 412...Packed 1 dozen to a carton. Shipping weight 29 lbs. per carton. Terms: 2% 10 days E. O. M., F. O. B. Culver City. Regular trade discounts. Newspaper mats available.

Representatives
Jalof & Lewis, 1110 Wilshire Blvd., Los Angeles 14, Calif.
Toy Market, 1424 Merchandise Mart, Chicago 54, Illinois
A. J. Frank, 200 Fifth Avenue, New York 10, New York
Russell D. Jesse Co., 644 Blvd., N. E., Atlanta, Georgia

created by A Futurland Toy MATTEL

Mattel Creations 8434-36 Warner Drive, Culver City, California

Hickory Dickory Musical CLOCK

A MATTEL *"Mousterpiece"*

NO. 456

Brilliant 4-color illustration litho'd on metal. Plated plastic bell. Plays "Hickory Dickory Dock" as crank is turned. "When the clock strikes One" …the sleeping cat's eyes pop open…the bell rings, jumps up and uncovers the hidden mouse.

DING

—Educational…movable hands teach children to tell time.

Size: 8¼" x 7" x 3"
Packed 2 doz. to carton
Ship. wt. approx. 17 lbs.

OPPOSITE: Sell sheet for the Futurland Grand Piano, 1951.
ABOVE: The Hickory Dickory Musical Clock, from the Mattel Music Makers Catalog, Fall 1952.
FOLLOWING PAGES: The Ducky Parade Pull Toy, from the Mattel Music Makers Catalog, Spring 1952.

Size: 2⅜ x 5⅛ x 11½
Packed 2 doz. to a carton
Ship. wt. approx. 11½ lbs.

No. 451

DUCKY

PARADE

Three playful
crew caps.
and blue whe
BUY count

(A *Mattel Pull Toy*)

c moulded ducks, complete with multi-colored
follow-the-leader as they waddle on red, green
ackaged in a rib-tickling duotone color, EYE-
play package.

Sell sheet for the Cowboy Ge-tar Music Box, 1951.

Sell sheet for the Dancing Dude Music Box, 1951.

Jack in the MUSIC BOX

The music plays "Pop Goes the Weasel." POP goes the top—UP jumps Mr. Jolly Tune, the clown —Up go sales on Mattel Music Maker Toys!

Patent Pending

Packed 2 doz. to carton. Shipping wt. approx. 31 lbs. Terms: 2% 10 days E. O. M. F. O. B. Culver City. Regular trade discounts. Newspaper mats and electros available.

Mattel Has the Secret

A new "surprise" version of an old favorite toy. Sturdily constructed with brilliant full-color lithographed decor designed with rare imagination by Bob Routledge.

Representatives:
Jalof & Lewis . . . 1110 Wilshire Blvd., Los Angeles 14, Calif.
Toy Market . . . 1424 Merchandise Mart, Chicago 54, Illinois
A. J. Frank . . . 200 Fifth Avenue, New York 10, New York
Russell D. Jesse Co. . . . 644 Blvd., N.E., Atlanta 5, Georgia

A MATTEL *Music Maker Toy*

Metal-reinforced box, 5⅜" square, 5¾" tall. Spring steel mechanism, metal pop-up lid. *Mr. Jolly Tune* is plastic clown, in ruffled polka dot clothing and perky hat. Priced for volume sales. **No. 430.**

Mattel Creations

8436 WARNER DRIVE, CULVER CITY, CALIF.

HE WHIRLS

HE'S UPSIDE
DOWN

UP . . . UP AND OVER.
START HIM AGAIN.

MUSICAL MAN ON THE
FLYING TRAPEZE

STOCK #468

. . . Turn the crank, listen to the music of
"The Daring Young Man on the Flying
Trapeze" and watch him float through the
air! Gay circus figures and the words of the
song litho'd on metal in rich 4 color art
work. Rugged ALL-METAL construction.

*Turn crank, acrobat begins
fancy tricks as music plays.*

*Packaged in individ-
ual, corrugated box.
Full color label.
Only one simple
part to assemble.*

MUSICAL MAN
ON THE
FLYING TRAPEZE

A MATTEL MUSIC MAKER TOY

Size: Overall height 21"
Packed: 1 doz. per std. ship. ctn.
Weight: Approximately 22 lbs.

Mattel, Incorporated — 5432 West 102nd St., Los Angeles 45, Calif.

OPPOSITE: Sell sheet for the Jack in the Music Box, 1951.
ABOVE: The Musical Man on the Flying Trapeze music box, from the Mattel Catalog, 1953.
FOLLOWING PAGES: Mattel's first toy vehicle, the Mattel Dream Car, from the Mattel Catalog, 1953.

THE MATTEL *Dream Car*

STOCK #465

The only car of its kind in the world of toys

The famed BOM[...]
transpare[...]
Snap — and the[...]
Snap — and the[...]
Just as simple [...]

- *Ahead of its time in design and conception.*
  - *Ahead of its time in dream-lined perfection.*

Low slung, impact resistant plastic body. Permanent, high gloss chrome trim. BOMBER BUBBLE transparent convertible top. SPEED STREAK friction motor. 4 futuristic colors. Individually packed in eye catching 3 color box.

PATENT NOS. 2,504,666—2,630,655—OTHERS PEND.

...BBLE
...ble top.
...s off.
...again.

Dream Car silver and gold trim is specially plated hi-polished chrome.

As permanent as it is beautiful. Slick shine sets off dream-line styling of tomorrow.

Car Size: 10½" long x 2¾" high x 5" wide.
Packed: *Assorted colors.* Std. two doz. carton
Shipping Weight: Approx. 21 lbs. per carton

RED BLAZE

BLUE BULLET

CHARTREUSE DREAMLINER

BLACK DIAMOND

Hold car firmly, give Speed Streak friction motor a quick push. As wheels revolve, let Dream Car speed away.

Incorporated — 5432 West 102nd St., Los Angeles 45, Calif.

Mattel Incorporated

TOY MAKERS · 5432 WEST 102nd STREET · LOS ANGELES 45, CALIFORNIA

M MUSIC **A** ACTION **C** COLOR

SPRING 1954

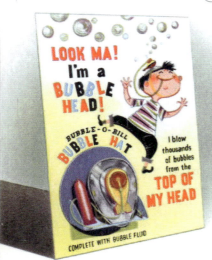

**LOOK MA!
I'm a
BUBBLE
HEAD!**

I blow thousands of bubbles from the **TOP OF MY HEAD**

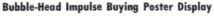

Bubble-Head Impulse Buying Poster Display
Easel backed, heavy cardboard. For counter or window.
Displays Bubble Hat and Fluid.
SIZE: 14" x 22" (FREE with each standard carton).

BUBBLE-O-BILL BUBBLE HAT
#479

Toyland's NEWEST sensation.
Blows thousands of bubbles OFF
THE TOP OF YOUR HEAD.

Complete with shining aluminum
space hat, spill-proof bubble
pipe, 22-inch safety vinyl mouth
tube and 2 packages bubble
fluid. Makes hours of bubble-
head blowing. Works well with
ANY fluid.

SIZE: 6" long x 2" wide x 2" high.
PACKED: 3 dozen per standard carton.
APPROXIMATE WEIGHT: 18 pounds.

BUBBLE-O-BILL
BUBBLE PIPE
#459

One pipe and one foil package of
bubble fluid individually packaged
in colorful, eye-catching display
box. Easy to stock, easy to sell!

SIZE OF DISPLAY CARTON: 6" x 6" x 1½".
PACKED: 4 dozen per standard carton.
APPROXIMATE WEIGHT: 12 pounds.

Works well with ANY bubble fluid.

**Bubble-O-Bill
Special
Display Pack**
#469

Works well with
ANY bubble fluid.

Two dozen pipes (without fluid). Packaged in
three-color display box. Bagged individually in
printed transparent package.
SIZE: 10½" front x 9½" deep x 5" high.
PACKED: Three display packs (2 dozen each pack) to
standard shipping carton.
APPROXIMATE WEIGHT: 5½ pounds.

THE *NEW*
MATTEL MERRY MUSIC BOX
#501

All metal—will last a lifetime! Gay litho'd
on metal four-color artwork. Assorted tunes.
Over-the-shoulder carrying cord. Individually boxed in eye-catching duo-colored
chipboard.

SIZE: 8" x 6" x 2".
PACKED: 2 dozen per standard shipping carton.
APPROXIMATE WEIGHT: 20 pounds per standard carton.

Patent Nos. 2,504,666 and 2,630,655   Others pending.

ABOVE: The Bubble-O-Bill toy range, and the Merry Music Box, from the Music Color Action Catalog, Spring 1954.
OPPOSITE: The Prince Valiant Sword, Scabbard, and Shield set, from the Music Color Action Catalog, Fall 1954.

Prince Valiant
SWORD, SCABBARD & SHIELD

Stock #506   List Price $3.00 (per set)   Fair Trade minimum $2.98

Stock up to take advantage of local promotional tie-ups with 20th Century Fox film "Prince Valiant" due for national theatre release around Easter. Watch for the play date in your city.

NO SHARP POINTS! NO DANGEROUS METALS!

SAFETY...Stay-on soft rubber sword tip. Sparkle-Shine flexible blade.

BEAUTY...Jeweled GOLD-GLO Sword Handle.

DRAMATIC, ALL-METAL WARRIOR SHIELD...

All rolled edges. 12" in diameter. Authentic Prince Valiant reproduction litho'd in 4 colors. Vinyl Holding Straps.

4 Color combination POINT-OF-SALE Display Box and Gift Package.

SIZE: Sword 18" long, Shield 12" diameter.
PACKED: ½ doz. individually boxed sets in std. shipping carton.
WEIGHT: 9 lbs. std. shipping carton.

Stock #505
List Price $2.00
Fair Trade minimum $1.98

A Safe, Beautiful, Authentic Sword. 18 inches long.
Litho'd 4 color metal, belt hanging scabbard. All rolled edges.

PACKED: 1 doz. individually boxed Sword & Scabbard sets to EACH 4 color POINT-OF-SALE Display carton. 2 Display cartons in std. shipping carton.
WEIGHT: 13 lbs. per std. shipping carton.

FLEXIBLE Sword blade. Bends almost double without breaking. IT'S SAFE for all ages.

Stay-on Soft rubber Sword Tip.

SAFE—Even for the youngest KNIGHT at your ROUND TABLE.

Copyright by King Features Syndicate Inc.

MATTEL INC. SPRING CATALOGUE 1955

EASTER EGG MUSIC BOX

STOCK #513
LIST $1.00   FAIR TRADE MIN. $.98

SUPER RABBIT SIZED, ALL-METAL, "TUFF-TO-BREAK" MUSICAL EASTER EGG. Patented music box plays gay assorted tunes. Four holiday designs color-litho'd on metal. Size: 6" High.

PACKED AND SHIPPED IN 2 COLOR EGG-CRATED DISPLAY CARTON, COMPLETE WITH MULTI-COLOR, PRICE MARKED DISPLAY CARD AND DUAL-PURPOSE ADVERTISING STREAMER.

PACKED: 1 DOZ. TO DISPLAY CARTON.   SHIPPING WEIGHT: 6 LBS.   17 DOZ.—100 LBS.

PETER COTTONTAIL MUSICAL EASTER BASKET

STOCK #698
LIST $1.00   FAIR TRADE MIN. $.98

Four color litho candy-packed, music-packed, Easter basket. Plays real Peter Cottontail music when crank is turned. Filled with colored Easter eggs heat-sealed in sanitary, cellophane package. Size: 5" Tall.

PACKED: INDIVIDUALLY PACKED IN 2 COLOR CHIP. SLEEVE.
2 DOZ. TO STANDARD CARTON.

WEIGHT: 15 LBS. PER CORRUGATED SHIP. CARTON. 14 DOZ.—100 LBS.

#798 WITHOUT CANDY
INDIV. PACKED IN PLAIN GRAY CHIPBOARD SLEEVE

PACKED: 2 DOZ.   WEIGHT: 10 LBS.   20 DOZ.—100 LBS.

Patent Nos. 2,504,666 and 2,630,655   Others pending.   Patented in Canada 1953   (OVER)

The Easter Egg Music Box and Peter Cottontail Musical Easter Basket, from the Mattel Catalog, Spring 1955.

#534 *List $2*
MOUSEKARTOONER

The MOUSEKARTOONER is a cartooning toy. Children simply trace the lines of any Disney character, any cartoon or picture and its copy appears double the size like magic. All metal base with full-color reproduction of Big Mouseketeer Roy Williams cartooning . . . just like he does it on the show. With drawing pad, pencil and full packet of Disney characters. Individually packed in two-color box. *$2.00*
Size: 15" x 9" x 1". Std. Pack: 1 doz. Approx. Wt: 12 lbs.*
©*Copyright Walt Disney Productions*

FALL '56

MATTEL, INC.
TOYMAKERS
M
MICKEY MOUSE CLUB

A MICKEY MOUSE CLUB THEATER "at home"

©*Copyright Walt Disney Productions*

MICKEY MOUSE CLUB NEWSREEL
with sound* *Stock #533   List $3 (batteries not included)*

Just insert a film slide into this battery-operated "tuff-to-break" projector and see Walt Disney films . . . on a 12 x 9 screen, at home. Projector has focusing lens, metal tripod, with polyethylene tips, push-button film advance. Two 10-frame film slides come with a non-breakable 78 RPM record with vocal and musical descriptions. Colorfully packaged toy includes projector, screen, slides and record.
Size: Projector: 9¼ x 5½ x 4. Std. Pack: 6/12 doz. Wt: 4 lbs.

MICKEY MOUSE CLUB NEWSREEL RECORD-FILM DOUBLE FEATURE *Stock #541*

List $.50 (1 record and 2 ten-picture film slides packed in envelope)

24 assorted records and 48 film slides packed in attractive point-of-sale display box. Assorted Disney subjects: cartoons, adventures, newsreels. Std. pack 6 doz. records. (3 displays per carton) Wt: 6 lbs.

MICKEY MOUSE CLUB NEWSREEL INTRODUCTORY DEAL

Stock #542
Retail Value $30.00
Consists of: 1 ea. #541 Record Library (24 assorted records, 48 film slides). 6 ea. #533 Newsreel (includes toy, screen, record and film slides). 1 ea. large point-of-sale display. Order by the Deal! Std. Pack: 1 ea. Wt: 6 lbs.

Mattel patented musical unit

©*Copyright Walt Disney Productions*

MOUSEGETAR—IN TWO SIZES! YOU'LL SEE JIMMIE DODD PLAY IT ON THE MICKEY MOUSE CLUB TV SHOW!

Stock #532 MOUSEGETAR JR.

Turn the crank of this Mattel music box, and play the official "Mouseketeer" song! Bright four-color decoration of Mickey and his friends on the face of the toy. Sturdy "tuff-to-break" construction. Nylon strumming strings, black-and-white neck cord. Individually packaged in colorful chipboard box.
List $1.80 Size: 14" x 5" x 1½". Std. Pack: 2 dozen
Stock #532 Approx. Wt.: 12 pounds

MOUSEGETAR *Stock #531*

Just like Jimmie Dodd's—plays real music! Seniormouse size, with nylon strings, tuning keys, carrying cord. Sturdy "tuff-to-break" construction. Bright red with Mickey Mouse Face. Jimmie's own instruction book teaches MICKEY MOUSE CLUB songs easily. Individually packaged in carrying case.
Size: 23" long x 8⅛" wide x 2½" deep. Std. Pack: 6/12 doz. Approx. Wt.: 10 pounds; Stock #531 List $4

Another Mickey Mouse Club TV toy

The Mousegetar and other Mickey Mouse Club toys, from the Mattel Catalog, Fall 1956. Mattel began selling Mickey Mouse toys in 1955, coinciding with the brand's pioneering sponsorship of *The Mickey Mouse Club* television program.

CATALOG 1957

FISHER · PRICE
TOYS

Fisher · Price Toys, Inc.

Main Office: East Aurora, Erie County, N. Y.   •   New York Office: 200 Fifth Avenue Bldg.   •   Chicago Office: The Merchandise Mart

ABOVE: The Fisher-Price Toys Catalog, 1957.
OPPOSITE: The Pull-a-Tune Xylophone and Roller Chime, from the Fisher-Price Toys Catalog, 1957.

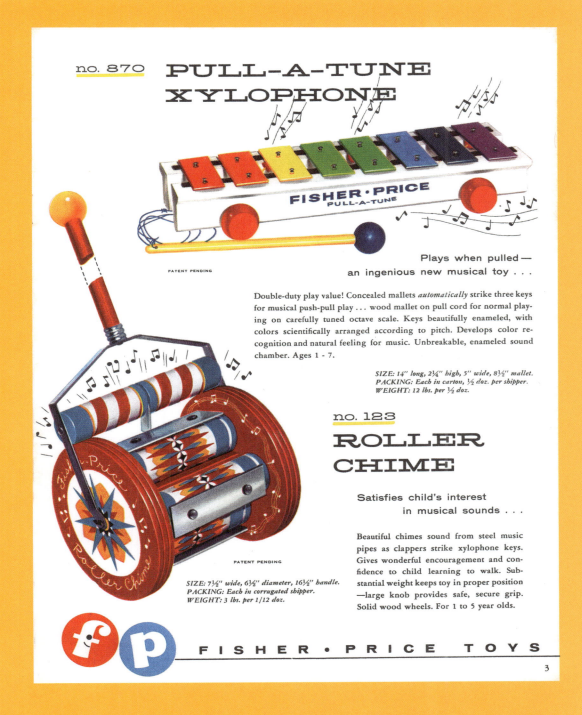

no. 870

PULL-A-TUNE XYLOPHONE

FISHER·PRICE PULL-A-TUNE

PATENT PENDING

Plays when pulled —
an ingenious new musical toy . . .

Double-duty play value! Concealed mallets *automatically* strike three keys for musical push-pull play . . . wood mallet on pull cord for normal playing on carefully tuned octave scale. Keys beautifully enameled, with colors scientifically arranged according to pitch. Develops color recognition and natural feeling for music. Unbreakable, enameled sound chamber. Ages 1 - 7.

SIZE: 14" long, 2¼" high, 5" wide, 8½" mallet.
PACKING: Each in carton, ½ doz. per shipper.
WEIGHT: 12 lbs. per ½ doz.

no. 123

ROLLER CHIME

Satisfies child's interest
in musical sounds . . .

Beautiful chimes sound from steel music pipes as clappers strike xylophone keys. Gives wonderful encouragement and confidence to child learning to walk. Substantial weight keeps toy in proper position —large knob provides safe, secure grip. Solid wood wheels. For 1 to 5 year olds.

PATENT PENDING

SIZE: 7½" wide, 6½" diameter, 16½" handle.
PACKING: Each in corrugated shipper.
WEIGHT: 3 lbs. per 1/12 doz.

F I S H E R · P R I C E   T O Y S

3

Fisher-Price was founded in 1930 during the Great Depression by Herman Fisher, Irving and Margaret Evans Price, and Helen Schelle, who all believed it was essential to create toys that contributed to children's development and learning, while also maintaining a sense of playfulness and fun.

The founders were able to raise over $100,000 in local capital from within their East Aurora, New York village to get started, popularizing the fundamental toy-making principles that centered on intrinsic play value, ingenuity, strong construction—early toys were made of heavy steel parts and ponderosa pine—and affordability. Fisher-Price presented sixteen toys at the Toy Show in New York City in 1931 and posted its first profit within six years. Starting in 1961, Fisher-Price began inviting local kids to their Play Lab—a dedicated research center to test out new toy prototypes—and introduced a corresponding Play Family product line, which was eventually renamed Little People.

In 1993, Mattel bought Fisher-Price and, over the next four years, established the brand as the home for all its preschool products. Since then, Fisher-Price has claimed the title of number-one infant and pre-school company in the world—the only kids' brand focused solely on ages 0–5.

MATTEL MODERN

FALL 1958

DOLL FURNITURE FOR 8" TO 10½" DOLLS

Cover and pages from the Mattel Modern Catalog, 1958.
The Mattel Modern range was a set of wooden modernist furniture made in Japan.

STUDIO SET

STUDIO BED
Stock #811   Retail Price: $2.50

Stock #810   Retail Price $6.00
Two convertible sofa beds, table
and lamp. Beds come with 2
upholstered bolsters and foam
mattress. Battery operated lamp
(battery not included.) (FOR
8″ DOLL ONLY)

DINING ROOM SET

Stock #815   Retail Price: $6.50
Modern dining table with two
upholstered chairs and buffet (4
drawers, sliding door and
shelves). Buffet or table with
chairs available separately.

NEW! MONKEY-O-LA *T.M.

579

Stock #579   Retail Price: $3

Turn the crank, play a merry tune. Watch the monkey bow and tip his hat. All-metal music box, gaily decorated with mechanical monkey attached. Shoulder carrying cord. Individually packaged in self-display box.

Size: 7¾" x 2⅛" x 10" (including Monkey)
Std. Pack: 6/12 doz.   Wt: 8 lbs.

Mattel patented musical unit

Mattel patented musical unit

NEW! TIPPEE TIM T.M.
THE DANCING MONKEY

580

Stock #580   Retail Price: $6

Turn the crank, play a tune. Monkey dances, tips his hat and jiggles coin cup. Circus-size, all-metal music box gaily litho'd. Plush mechanical monkey with colorful costume. Individually packaged box, containing self-display tray.

Size: Music Box: 10" x 8" x 4"; Monkey: 8"
Std. Pack: 6/12 doz.   Wt: 17½ lbs.

578

Walt Disney's
MOUSECLUBOUSE
TREASURE BANK

Stock #578   Retail Price: $2

A new personal hideaway bank built as an exact replica of the famous Mouseketeer Club House shown daily on the Mickey Mouse Club TV Show . . . center of fun for Jimmie Dodd and all the gang. Comes with 2 realistic hideaway keys for secret vault. Slot in the roof for deposits without opening door. Sturdy, tuff-to-break plastic, all metal, litho'd in four colors. Individually boxed.

Size: 8" x 5½" x 6½"
Std. Pack: 1 doz.   Wt: 11 lbs.

Holds thousands of coins

© Copyright Walt Disney Productions

490

MUSIC MAKER BOOKS

Stock #490   Retail Price: $1.20

Turn the crank . . . each book plays its own story in music. Color illustrations and rhymes. One dozen in each display pack consisting of 12 assorted titles. Two new titles: "Row, Your Boat", "If I Were A Cowboy."

Size: 6¾" x 5" x 1"
Std. Pack: 3 doz. (3 display packs)   Approx. Wt: 14 lbs.

Mattel patented musical unit

Assorted musical toys and the Mouseclubouse Treasure Bank, from the Mattel Catalog, Fall 1958.

NEW!

MATTEL POWERARM T.M. BARBELLS

POWERARM T.M. BARBELLS— OLYMPIC SET

Stock #591   Retail Price: $7
Complete physical fitness equipment for
the junior athlete — barbells and dumbells.
Just fill the leak-proof weights with
water or sand to vary weight from 2 lbs. to
20 lbs. Complete with 6 (two 8" and
four 5⅜") safe, non-marring polyethylene
weights; one 32" aluminum bar; two
10½" aluminum bars; 14 lock nuts; and
instruction sheet. Individually packaged.
*Size: Two 8" weights; four 5⅜" weights, and
one 32" bar; two 10½" bars*
Std. Pack: 6/12 doz. Wt: 23 lbs.

POWERARM T.M. BARBELLS— PROFESSIONAL SET

Stock #590   Retail Price: $5
For boys and girls! Exciting, new, safe method for body and muscle building.
Just fill the leak-proof weights with water or sand to vary weight from
2 lbs. to 16 lbs. Complete with 4 (two 8" and two 5⅜") safe, non-marring poly-
ethylene weights; one 32" aluminum bar; 5 lock nuts; and
instruction sheet. Individually packaged.
Size: Two 8" weights; two 5⅜" weights; and one 32" bar
Std. Pack: 6/12 doz. Wt: 16½ lbs.

The Powerarm Barbells Olympic and Professional sets, from the Mattel Catalog, Fall 1958.

"*Barbie always represented the fact that* **a woman has choices.**"

Ruth Handler, from her 1994 autobiography *Dream Doll: The Ruth Handler Story*

CHAPTER TWO

Big Dreams Lead to Big Brands

Mattel had made a big name for itself in a very short timeframe when Ruth Handler had an idea that would boost the company onto the global stage.

Ruth had long been inspired by her daughter, Barbara, who loved playing with paper dolls. Barbara and her friends pretended that their paper dolls had grown-up jobs, grown-up wardrobes, and grown-up lives. While on a vacation in Germany, Ruth spotted Bild Lilli dolls, grown-up novelty dolls based on a comic and marketed to adults. Ruth had been trying for some time to persuade Mattel's designers to create an adult doll, and now she had an example of how it could be done.

1959–1969

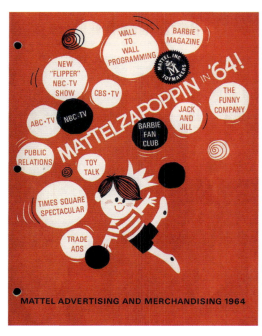

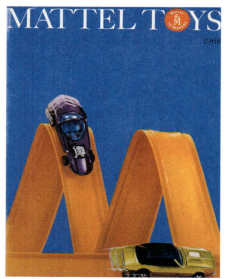

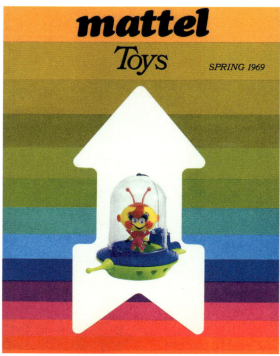

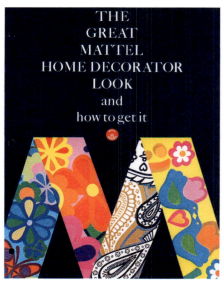

The result was Barbie, named after Ruth's daughter. Barbie was a plastic doll with moveable limbs. She had grown-up curves, a fashionable array of detailed and finely finished clothes, accessories that would be sold separately, and she would go on to hold a number of grown-up jobs. She also represented a big risk for Mattel.

At first, Barbie wasn't the slam dunk Ruth had envisioned: the doll's curves were considered too risqué by mothers, ad executives, and even many of Mattel's own employees, and her clothes were expensive to produce. But Ruth refused to back down, even when Barbie Teen-Age Fashion Model's debut at 1959's New York City Toy Fair was a flop. But Ruth believed she had something incredible all along, and she was right: later that same year, girls embraced Barbie wholeheartedly, with 351,000 Barbie dolls sold. Mattel scrambled to ramp up the production they'd reduced since toy buyers—almost entirely men—had refused to purchase the dolls upon debut, but it still took three years to fully catch up with demand.

The success of Barbie gave Mattel the push it needed to become a publicly traded company in 1960, and, within five years, Mattel was listed on the New York Stock Exchange. The value of Mattel shares rose fifty percent over the course of a decade, making Mattel an investor's darling.

With investors on board and profits climbing steadily, Mattel had the capital to invest in new technology. They soon had another hit on their hands with Chatty Cathy, a toy perfect for girls who were too old for baby dolls, but weren't quite ready for Barbie. Chatty Cathy was the company's first in a line of interactive models that could speak recorded words and phrases when a string was pulled in their backs. In 1965, Mattel used the same technology to create educational toys for the pre-school set with the See 'n Say, a toy that could call out the names and sounds of the animals on its colorful façade. It was immediately popular and remains a consistent seller for Mattel even today.

Mattel had cornered the market for girls, but they really wanted to create a toy line for boys with the same evergreen appeal as Barbie. They tried action figures with some success, but found their breakthrough with Hot Wheels cars. In 1968 Mattel raced out of the gate with sixteen 1:64 scale model die-cast cars with moving wheels and working axels. The mini cars, designed in flashy California custom car culture colors, were an instant hit because they could actually race, unlike other die-cast cars on the market. It's Mattel lore that Elliot himself named the cars after seeing them rolling along the hallway, when he said, "Those are some hot wheels!" And they were hot. Mattel sold $25 million worth of Hot Wheels in 1968.

As the 1960s drew to a close, Mattel had reached a level of success that the Handlers never thought possible when they began. Mattel was officially the world's most successful toymaker.

OPPOSITE, CLOCKWISE FROM UPPER LEFT: Mattel catalog covers from 1969, 1964, 1959, 1965, 1969, 1970, and 1966. The Barbie catalog shown here marked the announcement of Barbie's creation in 1959.

Catalog Archive

ABOVE: The first appearance of the Chatty Cathy doll, from the Mattel Dolls Catalog, 1960.
FOLLOWING PAGES: Barbie fashion sets and a promotional 7" record featuring the "voices" of Barbie and Ken, from the Mattel Dolls Catalogs, 1960 and 1961. Barbie made her debut in 1959 and appeared in a catalog for the first time in 1960.

WEDDING DAY
Stock #972. Retail: $5.00

SILKEN FLAME
Stock #977. Retail: $1.50

FASHION UNDERGARM
Stock #919. Retail: $

Barbie*

TEEN-AGE FASHION MODEL

NEW FASHION APPEAL FOR GIRLS OF ALL AGES!

An exciting, all-new kind of doll...she's shapely and grown-up...so curvy and lifelike, she almost breathes. She stands alone. Girls of all ages will thrill to her miniature wardrobe of fine-fabric fashions: tiny zippers...coats with luxurious, tailored linings...jeweled earrings, necklaces and color-coordinated sun glasses!

COSTUMES (without dolls) AND ACCESSORIES — individually packaged as below and described on the following two pages.

BARBIE*   **TEEN-AGE FASHION MODEL**

TV ADVERTISED

STOCK #850. Retail $3.00. Sturdy, vinyl plastic. Movable arms, legs and head for easy dressing. Rooted Saran hair, plus jersey swimsuit, sun glasses, earrings and shoes...pedestal. Size: 11½" tall. Std. Pack: 1 doz. (8 blonde, 4 brunette). Wt., 8½ lbs.

*Barbie, T.M. MCMLVIII by Mattel, International

NEW GIFT PAKS

PARTY SET

STOCK #856. Retail Price: $10.00. Complete ensembles for tonight's party...this afternoon's shopping. Basic Barbie* Teen-Age Fashion Model doll, plus: (1) Plantation Belle dress, slip, straw hat, bra and pants; (2) Suburban Shopper dress, Silken Flame dress and belt, Golden Girl dress, "pearl" necklace, gold purse. Std. Pack: 6/12 doz. Wt., 13 lbs.

MIX 'N MATCH SET

Stock #857. Retail Price: $12.00. For Barbie* at play ...and Barbie* at work. Basic Barbie* doll, plus: (1) Winter Holiday leather jacket and hooded T-shirt; Resort Set jacket and hat; Picnic Set Levis and blouse; sleeveless sweater; (2) Sweater Girl sweater and skirt; shorts, T-shirt; blouse; Winter Holiday leotard, shoes, valise; Fashion Undergarments bra and panties; crystal necklace. Std. Pack: 6/12 doz. Wt. 13¾ lbs.

TROUSSEAU SET

STOCK #858. Retail Price: $20.00. Everything for the wedding...and the honeymoon too. Basic Barbie* doll, plus: (1) Silken Flame dress, Sweater Girl sleeveless sweater, negligee, gown and peignoir, slippers, brush, comb, mirror; (2) Cotton Casual dress, Resort Set blouse, jacket and shorts, Winter Holiday leotard, alarm clock, cork shoes; (3) Evening Splendour dress, coat, gloves, purse and hat box, Commuter Set suit, white blouse and pants, bra, girdle, panty, "pearl" necklace and bracelet, handkerchief; (4) Wedding gown, veil, blue garter, bouquet, wedding shoes. Std. Pack: 6/12 doz. Wt., 16¾ lbs.

LET'S DANCE
Stock #978. Retail: $2.00

FRIDAY NITE DATE
Stock #979. Retail: $2.50

GOLDEN GIRL
Stock #911. Retail: $

WINTER HOLIDAY
Stock #975. Retail: $

RESORT SET Stock #963. Retail: $2.50	PEACHY FLEECY COAT Stock #915. Retail: $2.50	SUBURBAN SHOPPER Stock #969. Retail: $2.50	NIGHTY-NEGLIGEE SET Stock #965. Retail: $3.00	SWEATER GIRL Stock #976. Retail: $3.00	EVENING SPLENDOR Stock #961. Retail: $4.00

BALLERINA Stock #989. Retail: $3.00	REGISTERED NURSE Stock #991. Retail: $3.00	OPEN ROAD Stock #985. Retail: $3.50	SWEET DREAMS Stock #973. Retail: $1.25	PICNIC SET Stock #967. Retail: $2.50	FLORAL PETTICOAT Stock #921. Retail: $1.25

BARBIE-Q OUTFIT Stock #962. Retail: $2.00	SINGING IN THE SHOWER Stock #988. Retail: $2.00	COTTON CASUAL Stock #912. Retail: $1.00	SHEATH SENSATION Stock #986. Retail: $1.50	ORANGE BLOSSOM Stock #987. Retail: $2.50	AMERICAN AIRLINES STEWARDESS Stock #984. Retail: $3.50

Barbie® SINGS!

Now you can hear Barbie, too!

Stock #840. Retail Price: $3.00.

Now…to cap the fabulous Barbie line, comes a truly
irresistible addition…The Barbie Record Album…BARBIE SINGS!
6 smash-hit songs, on 3-45 rpm records! Barbie and Ken
come to life on these delightful records, singing 6 new
and original songs … "Nobody Taught Me" … "Ken" … "Barbie" …
"Instant Love"…"My First Date"…and "The Busy Buzz."
Swinging arrangements with a big band, perfectly
tailored for teen-age girls, with tender ballads, terrific jump tunes,
even a cha-cha number. Bound to be the smash hit of
the year with every Barbie fan…and every ten-thru-teen girl!

Size: 7¼" x 7¼". Std. Pack: 1 doz. Wt.: 6 lbs.

® Reg. Mattel, Inc., © 1961   TV ADVERTISED

MATTEL FALL 1961

you can tell it's Mattel...it's swell!

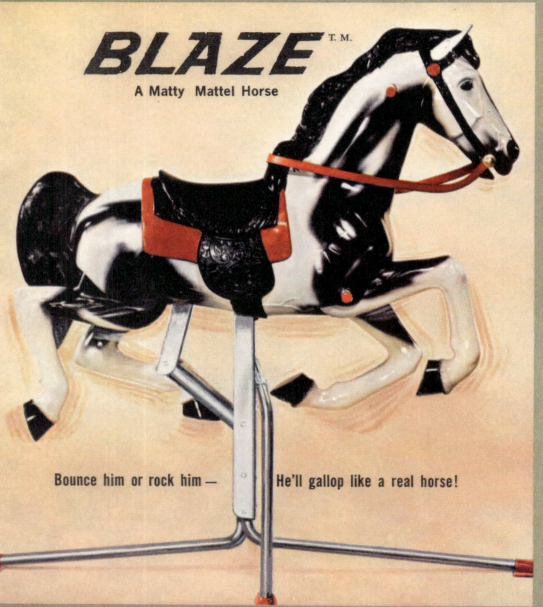

BLAZE T.M.
A Matty Mattel Horse

Bounce him or rock him — He'll gallop like a real horse!

Rock back and Blaze rears!

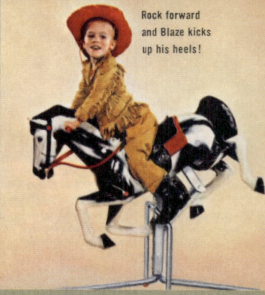

Rock forward and Blaze kicks up his heels!

BLAZE .. MATTEL'S FABULOUS NEW GALLOPING HOBBY HORSE

Stock #715. Retail Price $44.00

The only horse of its kind anywhere! All four legs move with realistic action when he's bounced up and down or rocked back and forth. Lean back, and Blaze rears at a safe angle; lean forward, and he kicks up his heels like a frisky colt! Blaze is the *biggest* hobby horse yet takes up less floor space because of his unique stand. And safe? There's none safer. The sturdy steel stand is already attached to Blaze and just won't tip, and the spring action is inside the horse, so a child cannot be pinched. (No exterior bar supports.) Blaze is a beautiful horse... gleaming black with white markings. He's realistically sculptured exactly like a real horse. Molded of Hi-impact plastic, with molded, black tooled saddle with a bright red saddle blanket and separate plastic reins. Fixed hand posts with two position foot rests.
THE ONLY HOBBY HORSE ADVERTISED ON TV
Size: Approximately 41" high (mounted on stand) x 36" long (nose to tail) *Std. Pack:* 1 ea. Wt.: 40 lbs.
® Reg. Mattel, Inc., Hawthorne, California T.M. © 1961 Patents Pending

MATTEL

NEW **POPzaBALL**™

A MATTEL ACTION TOY

POP ZA BALL

roll ball in—POPS right back

ROLL THE BALL IN...IT POPS RIGHT BACK!

POP ZA BALL target game

have a catch?

double-whammy

catch it on the run

invite a friend

follow the leader

POPZABALL TV ADVERTISED

Stock #714. Retail Price $7.00.

It's the brand new roll-and-catch action game with the fun built in. Just roll the ball in, and it automatically pops right back to you . . . so you can catch it on the fly. It's a natural for a dozen different games, perfect for boys and girls, indoors or out. One or more can play. Solidly constructed of Hi-impact plastic with 50-throw clock spring mechanism. Comes complete with 4 colorful plastic Popzaballs. Package target and full instruction booklet on how to play the many different Popzaball games.

Size: 11" x 9" x 15". Std. Pack: 4/12 doz. Wt.: 13 lbs.

T.M. © 1961 Mattel, Inc., Hawthorne, California

OPPOSITE: Blaze, a hobby horse set, from the Mattel Catalog, Fall 1961.
ABOVE: Popzaball, from the Mattel Catalog, Fall 1961.

DOLL AND CLOTHING NOT INCLUDED.

BARBIE'S® DREAM HOUSE

#816   Retail: $8.00

Barbie's Dream House is a proven sales dream, too! This patented Easy-to-Carry 3-color sturdy suitcase unfolds quickly and easily into three walls and the floor of Barbie's own house. Comes complete with custom-designed, easily assembled modern slim-line furniture, rugs and all the special decorative accessories Barbie has chosen for her home. All in sturdy, colorful chipboard. The house and all assembled furnishings fold away simply, neatly and compactly when not in use for easy portability and storage.

House size: 26"x 14½"x 33".
Std. Pack: 3/12 Doz.   Wt. 27 Lbs.
Shipped Garfield, New Jersey

EASY TO CARRY—
EASY TO STORE.

UNFOLD BARBIE'S
DREAM HOUSE.

EASY-TO-ASSEMBLE FURNITURE
AND FURNISHINGS.

34

ABOVE: The first appearance of Barbie's Dream House, in the Mattel Dolls Catalog, 1963.
OPPOSITE: The cover of the Mattel Dolls Catalog, 1963.

M
TV

HIGH-FASHION
WIGS—
3 DIFFERENT
COLORS—
3 DIFFERENT
STYLES
COMPLETE
WITH
WIG STAND

#870   Retail: $6.00

Girls of all ages will want super-sophisticated Fashion Queen Barbie! She comes with a new sculptured head and three high-fashion saran wigs in gorgeous colors, so her coiffure can change to go with different ensembles. Wigs are in three different styles—bubble-on-bubble, page boy and side-part flip. Wig stand holding all 3 included. Fashion Queen Barbie is dressed in her exclusive gold striped lamé swim suit, with matching beach hat, "pearl" earrings, white high-heeled shoes. Special wire stand included. All of the Barbie clothes fit her, too. Self-display see-through package. You can tell the genuine Fashion Queen Barbie by her identifying arm tag and her *unique* gold striped lamé swim suit.
Std. Pack: 1 Doz.   Wt. 9½ Lbs.

19

Fashion Queen Barbie, introduced in the Mattel Dolls Catalog, 1963.

Tiny Chatty Baby, Brother, and Twins dolls, from the Mattel Dolls Catalog, 1963.

Cheerful Tearful doll, from the Mattel Catalog, 1966.

RING-A-LING

EYES ROLL

PATENT PENDING

747 CHATTER TELEPHONE

The famous manipulative toy that answers the need for a play telephone designed specifically for preschool activity. When pulled along, "voice" says "chatter-chatter-chatter" and the eyes roll up and down. When dial is turned and released, bell rings. Unbreakable polyethylene receiver has new, spiral fabric cord. Sturdy wood and polyethylene base. An entertaining toy that is unusually effective for developing coordination, teaching colors and numbers, and for encouraging dramatic play. Boys and girls 2-6.

Size: 6½″ long, 4″ high, 7¼″ wide.
Packing: Each in window box,
1 doz. per 15 lb. shipper.

The Chatter Telephone, the Giant Rock-a-Stack, and the Corn Popper—three iconic toys from the Fisher-Price Catalog, 1962.

62

1959–1969

17

740 GIANT ROCK-A-STACK

The basic, always popular stacking toy in its finest design concept. Ten vividly colored rings are made of smooth polyethylene, are graduated in size to fit polyethylene cone in sequence of color spectrum. Removable ball holds rings on cone, cone unscrews from enameled wood rocker base. Unbreakable, chewable, washable, non-toxic. Correctly proportioned for preschool play. Develops color and shape perception, eye-hand coordination. Boys and girls 1-3.

Size: 5″ square base, 12¾″ high.
Packing: Each in display package, 1 doz. per 15 lb. shipper.

785 CORN POPPER

Push toy fascination as colorful wooden balls are hurled against see-through acetate dome with a "poppety-pop-pop" sound. Solid wood base, wheels and handle, beautifully enameled. Safe plastic push knob. Entrancing sound and action that encourages muscle building push toy play. Boys and girls 1-3.

Size: 6¼″ high, 6½″ wide, 18½″ handle.
Packing: Each in box, 1 doz. per 18 lb. shipper.

POP
POP
POP

CORN POPPER

FISHER · PRICE

PATENT NOS 2.835.074
2.833.063 2.747.328 2.937.475
DESIGN PATENT NO. 182.791
CANADIAN PATENT NOS
568.338 580.946 598.743
CAN R D 1958

FISHER-PRICE TOYS

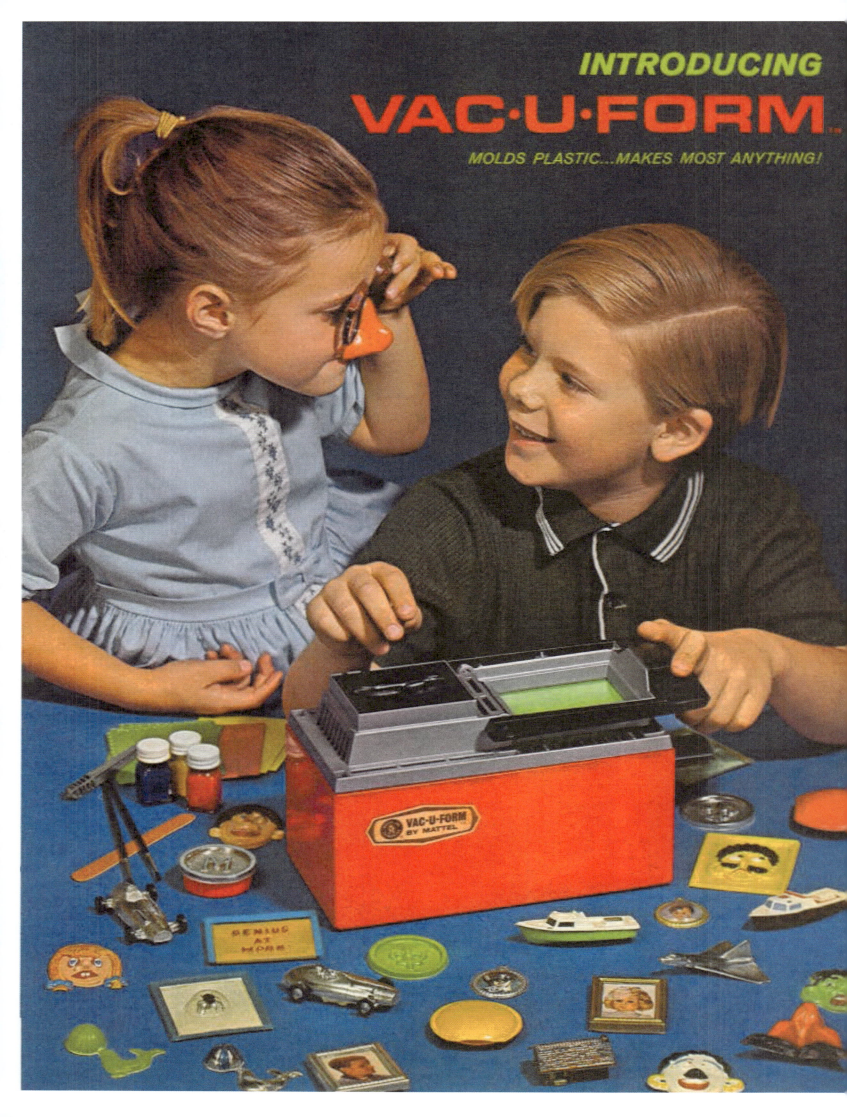

HIGH GEAR GAME

NEW!

A SENSATIONAL FAST-ACTION GAME FOR 2 TO 4 PLAYERS AGES SEVEN TO ADULT.
NO GAME PLAYS ALIKE...GEARS WHIRL IN 35,568 DIFFERENT PATTERNS!

TURN DIAL GEAR—ALL 10 GEARS SPIN SIMULTANEOUSLY.

#462   Retail: $6.00

Fun spins into "high gear" with this fascinating maneuver game based on an entirely new principle of play! Two to four players spin and dial each move on the Dial Gear, trying to guess which way all the gears will whirl to advance their pegs and send back "enemy" pegs! Object of the game is to race all four of your pegs from Gear No. 1 up to High Gear. To speed their pegs, players have lots of chances to "Turn High Gear" or "Hold the Clutch." Easy to learn, easy to play, this fast-moving game will delight both children and adults—just right for a family fun game. High Gear Game Board of high-impact plastic with multi-colored gears; 20 plastic pegs come stored in special sliding-door compartment; easy-to-follow illustrated instructions. Special self-sell "demonstration" package allows customer to "play" the game on the counter. Game size: 16" x 16".

Std. Pack: 6/12 Doz.   Wt. 23 lbs.

7

OPPOSITE: The Vac-u-Form plastic molding machine, from the Mattel Toys Catalog, 1963.
ABOVE: High Gear Game, from the Mattel Toys Catalog, 1963.
FOLLOWING PAGES: Spreads from the *Mattelzapoppin'* advertising brochure, 1964.

MATTEL® IS ON TV 6 DAYS A WEE[K]

IT WAS 3 NETWORKS IN '63...NOW MATTELZAPOPPIN' WITH A[

1 abc

"CASPER" 11.00   "BEANY & CECIL" 11:30

2 CBS TELEVISION NETWORK

"QUICK DRAW McGRAW" 10:00   "ROY ROGERS" 11:30

3 NBC

"FIREBALL XL-5" 10:30   "DENNIS THE MENACE" 11

4 the FUNNY COMPANY

A minimum number of stations may carry programs at time other than indicated.

The TV time listed is Eastern Standard.

Check your TV guide for local times.

"CASPER" ©Harvey Famous Cartoons

"BEANY" and "CECIL" ©1949, 1950, Robert E. (Bob) Clampett

"BUGS BUNNY" ©Warner Bros. Pictures, Inc.

The Funny Company characters ©1963 by The Funny Company, Inc.
All rights reserved throughout the world.

©1964 **MATTEL**, INC., Hawthorne, Calif. Printed in U.S.A.

"BUGS BUNNY" 12:00

"SKY KING" 12:00   "MY FRIEND FLICKA" 12:30

"FURY" 11:30   "EXPLORING" 12:00

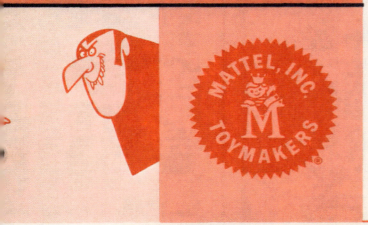

MATTEL'S WALL TO WALL PROGRAMMING BLANKETS SATURDAY MORNING ALL YEAR... AND INCREASES ITS DOMINATION WITH 11 SHOWS THIS FALL: 3 ON ABC, 4 ON NBC, 4 ON CBS! Virtually every child under 12 in your city will be seeing **Mattel's** award-winning, merchandise-moving commercials every single Saturday of the year. It's the most explosive network TV campaign ever put behind any toy line... and it really explodes this Fall, **when 9 out of every 10 network toy commercials between 11 A.M. and 12:30 P.M. will belong to Mattel.** There will be a total of 31 **Mattel** network commercials every Saturday this Fall, all concentrated during the peak kid-viewing hours of 10 A.M. to 1 P.M. And **Mattel's** network shows are seen in over 300 cities across the country... **covering more than 99% of all U.S. TV homes.**

MATTEL'S NEW 4TH NETWORK IS THE FUNNY COMPANY! AND IT'S ON EVERY WEEKDAY, ALL YEAR LONG! THE FUNNY COMPANY is now being shown on nearly 100 top-rated stations across the country. (With more being added every day.) On most of these stations, THE FUNNY COMPANY is on during the children's late afternoon viewing hours. THE FUNNY COMPANY has already won the admiration of parents, teachers, and children... because it combines the delightful cartoon adventures of the kids in THE FUNNY COMPANY with instructive live action segments explaining anything from "How Glass Is Made" to "What Makes Plants Grow." It's the newest, most entertaining children's show in a decade! **AND AGAIN IN '64 DURING YOUR PEAK FALL SELLING SEASON, MATTEL SPOT TV WILL SATURATE TOP-RATED CHILDREN'S SHOWS AND FAMILY PROGRAMS IN EVERY MAJOR MARKET IN THE COUNTRY!**

MATTELZAPOPPIN IN '64!

JACK & JILL MAGAZINE

Read each month by more than 1,700,000 boys, girls, and even parents, "Jack & Jill" is the largest and most respected children's publication in the country. And **Mattel's** schedule is really a blockbuster:

FULL PAGE 4-COLOR COVERS	2 PAGE SPREADS 4-COLOR
April	October
May	November
June	December
July	
August	
September	

And all the **Mattel** products advertised will be the only ones in their category appearing in the magazine.

you can tell it's **MATTEL** it's swell !!

beautiful shoes · Miller

TIMES SQUARE SPECTACULAR

It's the famous animated spectacular billboard in Times Square . . . the only one of its kind in the world! And **Mattel** is the only toy maker in the world ever to have a sign like this on the Great White Way. Next Fall, from October through December, millions of people from all over the country will see **Mattel's** selling message continuously . . . for 16 exciting hours every day!

BARBIE® MAGAZINE AND THE NATIONAL BARBIE FAN CLUB

Right now, there are over a quarter of a million members in **Mattel's** Official National **Barbie** Fan Club. And every single member is a pre-sold and ready-to-buy **Barbie** Fan! What's more, there are over 100,000 subscribers to the **Barbie** Magazine. They all look forward to every new issue . . . and to reading stories about **Barbie** and her friends, articles about distant lands, recipes, and ideas about special projects for **Barbie** Fan Club Chapters. (There are even contests in the **Barbie** Magazine . . . just for **Barbie** Fan Club members!) The **Barbie** Magazine gives extra exposure for the entire "World of **Barbie**" products 12 months a year!

PUBLIC RELATIONS

Mattel's sales and marketing efforts will receive again this year, as in the past, a major consumer informational program. This three-pronged campaign — publicity, promotion and public relations — will continue throughout the year. Through this program, stories and features about **Mattel** and its new toys will be placed with major magazines, newspapers and radio and television commentators to keep at a constant high level consumer interest in all the exciting new **Mattel** products, as well as the perennial best-sellers in the overall line.

TOY TALK

TOY TALK, a publication produced by **Mattel** for and about the toy merchant, will soon observe its third birthday. The two-color magazine, published bi-monthly, has gained considerable readership among toy retailers throughout the country since it was first introduced two years ago.

The purpose and goal of **TOY TALK** is to keep retailers up to date on new trends, unique promotions and interesting developments in our industry, as well as offer ideas and suggestions for building traffic and sales.

"BARBIE," is the registered trademark of Mattel, Inc., for its **teen-age doll.**

Introducing...The World of Kiddles

A special catalog announcing the debut of Kiddles, 1965.

Barbie fashion sets, including the first Astronaut Barbie, from the Mattel Catalog, Fall 1965.

NEW! SEE 'N SAY™ TOYS FUN FOR EVERY PRE-SCHOOLER...TOYS THAT TALK AND TEACH!

NEW! SEE 'N SAY THE FARMER SAYS
#4832

At last! A really exciting educational toy for children as young as 1½ years! Helps pre-schoolers learn to talk . . . to recognize animals . . . to learn the alphabet. Children rotate the pointer to the name and picture of an animal, then pull the CHATTY-RING® to hear farmer talk about the animal; for example: "The duck says quack, quack, quack!" Children can select any of twelve animal sayings with the pointer. Includes rooster, sheep, many more familiar animals. Hi-impact plastic, with carrying handle and stand-up base. No batteries needed.
Size: 12" x 10⅝" x 2⅝". Colorful picture-frame package.
Std. Pack: 6/12 Doz.   Wt. 12 Lbs.

NEW! SEE 'N SAY THE BEE SAYS #4831

It's a fascinating new way to learn the alphabet, because it's fun! Rotate the bee pointer to a familiar picture and a letter, then pull the CHATTY-RING®. The bee speaks the name of the picture and the letter: "Apple . . . A." All 26 letters of the alphabet are included, with a word for each! Child can rotate pointer to letter, or let the pointer select letters at random. Every parent is going to want one for his pre-schooler. Hi-impact plastic with carrying handle, stand up base. No batteries needed. 12" x 10⅝" x 2⅝". Colorful picture-frame package. Std. Pack: 6/12 Doz. Wt. 12 Lbs.

NEW! SEE 'N SAY ASSORTMENT #4829

4 ea. — SEE 'N SAY THE BEE SAYS #4831
4 ea. — SEE 'N SAY THE FARMER SAYS #4832
Std. Pack: 1 carton   Wt. 15½ Lbs.

35

The first See 'n' Say toys, from the Mattel Catalog, Fall 1965.

NEW!
LINOPRINTER^{T.M.}

#4400

AT LAST! A REVOLUTIONARY NEW PRINTING PRESS THAT KIDS WILL LOVE, PARENTS WILL APPROVE!
No more lost type, because the kids *make their own type* on continuous plastic tape — they can't run out of letters! No more spilled ink or mess, because the LINOPRINTER has a permanent ink supply built right into the roller. Never needs refilling! With 9 special printing plates, kids can have months of fun printing play money, newspapers, phony telegrams, license plates, badges, bulletins . . . almost anything! Constructed of metal and hi-impact plastic. The unique styrofoam package base guides papers into a neat stack as they're printed . . . and it comes with lots of paper, 2 rolls of plastic tape for type, 9 printing plates with borders and mastheads. Package size: 15" x 12⁷/₈" x 6¹/₄".
Std. Pack: 6/12 Doz.   Wt. 25 Lbs.

Dial a letter. Then press the handle to punch the letter onto the plastic tape. There's a complete alphabet with capital letters, numbers, and punctuation marks. Uses standard plastic embossing tape, available everywhere.

As each line is finished, press the adhesive-backed plastic tape on to the printing roller. When all the lines are in place, turn the roller to print. Type can be combined with the re-usable printing plates.

"LINOPRINTER" is the trademark of Mattel, Inc., for its TOY PRINTING PRESS

NEW! LINOPRINTER MERCHANDISER

#4403

Tells and sells the full LINOPRINTER story in attention-getting newspaper front-page format. Converts from counter unit to wall-mount.
Display size: 21" wide x 23" high x 19" deep.
Merchandise includes:
6 ea. — LINOPRINTER
1 ea. — DISPLAY
Std. Pack: 1 ea. (1 carton) Wt. 24 Lbs.

5

ABOVE: The Linoprinter printing press toy, from the Mattel Catalog, Fall 1965.
OPPOSITE: The V-rroom! line of bicycles, from the Mattel Catalog, Fall 1965.

"V-RROOM" is the registered trademark of Mattel, Inc.

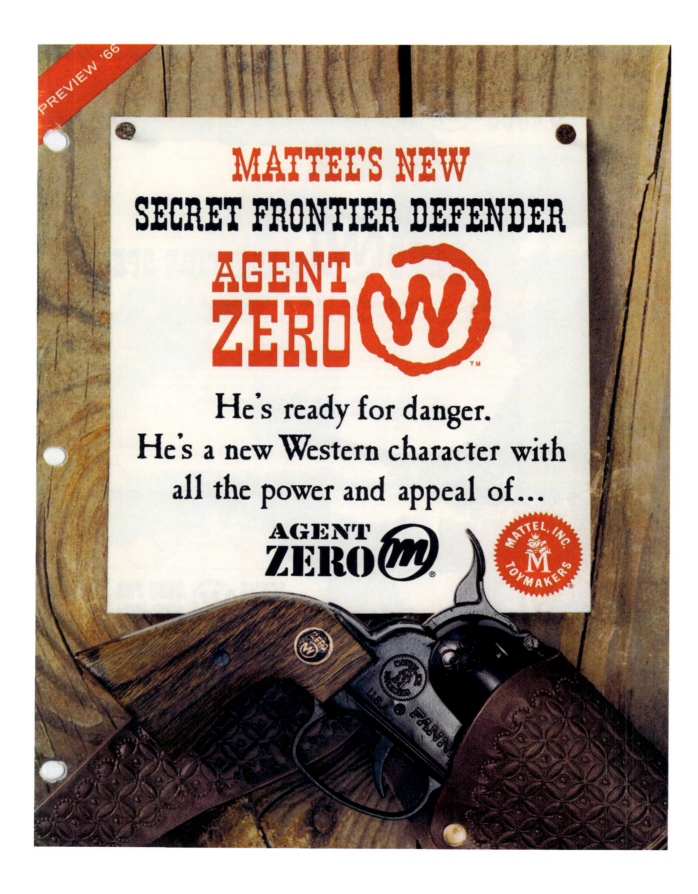

A special catalog announcing toy guns, holsters, and accessories for the new Western character Agent Zero, 1966.

AGENT ZERO W POTSHOT® AND WRIST HOLDER!

05

Every western agent must have something up his sleeve — the new POTSHOT Derringer and wrist holster (fits any wrist, arm or leg). Gleaming gold colored, embossed 3" Derringer shoots a SHOOTIN' SHELL® with GREENIE® STIK-M-CAP®. Holster with 13" strap has 2 SHOOTIN' SHELLS, and 6 safe bullet-noses.

Pilferproof new clear blister card packaging.

Std. Pack: 1 Doz.   Wt: 4 Lbs.

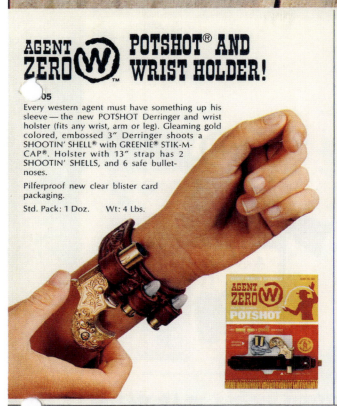

AGENT ZERO W BUCKLE GUN!

#5506

Even if they have him covered, an agent can fire the ZERO W Buckle Gun without moving a finger. A push of the stomach and a 3" Derringer pistol flips out of the nickel-colored engraved Western belt buckle...and automatically fires a GREENIE STIK-M-CAP and shoots a SHOOTIN' SHELL. All metal, 2½" x 4", fits any belt. The Derringer is removable. Safety lock prevents accidental firings. Complete with 2 SHOOTIN' SHELLS, 6 safe bullet-noses.

Pilferproof new clear blister card packaging.

Std. Pack: 1 Doz.
Wt: 6 Lbs.

Smoke Pours Out at Every Shot!

AGENT ZERO W NEW SMOKING FANNER-50® AND HOLSTER SETS!

Agent ZERO W SMOKING FANNER-50
#5502 Authentic fanning gun of the Old West — with a new look and realistic smoking action! Rapid-fans 50 Greenie perforated roll caps . . . fans or triggers single shots. Authentic gun metal color with gold-color cylinder and wood grain handle. 10¾" long. Sturdy die-cast construction.

Tray display package, 11" x 9" x 1¾".

Std. Pack: 1 Doz.   Wt: 11 Lbs.

Agent ZERO W SMOKING FANNER-50 SINGLE HOLSTER SET #5503 Basic for every western agent! Smoking Fanner-50 fires Greenie perforated roll caps with realistic smoking action. Adjustable belt and holster of rugged brown DURA-HYDE®.

Tray display package, 14½" x 8½" x 2½".

Std. Pack: 1 Doz.   Wt: 16 Lbs.

Agent ZERO W SMOKING FANNER-50 DOUBLE HOLSTER SET #5504 For twice the action, twice the fun! Two ZERO W SMOKING FANNER-50's...with two richly embossed, sturdy brown DURA-HYDE fast-draw holsters. Belt adjustable to any size child.

Tray display package 14½" x 11½" x 2½".

Std. Pack: 6/12 Doz.   Wt: 18½ Lbs.

LITHO IN U. S. A. © 1965 MATTEL, INC., HAWTHORNE, CALIFORNIA, U. S. A. ALSO AVAILABLE IN CANADA FROM MATTEL CANADA, LIMITED (A SUBSIDIARY OF MATTEL, INC.)

NEW AND REVOLUTIONARY!

Switch 'N Go

TV
PRINT

NEW! TWIN GT CAR SET #6112

- 2 CARS GO ANYWHERE — INDOORS OR OUT
- REMOTE AIR CONTROLS FOR THRILLING COMPETITION
- 60 FEET OF FLEXIBLE TRACK — HUNDREDS OF LAYOUTS

RACE THROUGH AUTOMATIC GATE CROSSING ...FLIP YOUR COMPETITOR...SWITCH CARS ANYWHERE AROUND TRACK. Press the Master Air Control — send a spurt of air through the hollow plastic track — activate Air Switches and Flip Crash trippers anywhere! Add extra track to control action hundreds of feet away! Track is flexible — cut it, join it, make it go in any direction. Change layouts over and over again. 3-speed racers run for hours on

one "D" battery (not included). 4 bridge sections permit crossovers and multilevel layouts. All components are rugged plastic. Includes: 2 GT Racers (1 red, 1 blue with custom trim kits), 2 Master Air Controls, Automatic Gate Crossing, 60-ft. of Track, 4 Bridge sections, Flip Crash, Air Flip Crash, 4 Y-Air Switches, 2 Cross-Overs, 2 Y-Connectors, Plugs, Joiners, Instructions. Package 26"x18"x4⅝" Std. Pack: 4/12 Doz. Wt: 18 Lbs.

MINIATURE CARS COLLECTORS' CASE
#7501

ALL NEW FOR '66, a quality vinyl case screened in miniature car motif, full color of course! Easy-end opening with two slide trays that hold 40 cars. A molded handle and snap fastener closure.

size: 13¼" x 8" x 3½"
packed: 1 doz. to ctn.
weight: 32 lbs. per ctn.
color: light orange screening on blue vinyl

Cars not included

OPPOSITE: Switch 'N' Go, a racecar and track set that used air from remote-controlled billows to drive the cars, from the Mattel Catalog, 1966.
ABOVE: Miniature Car Collector's Case, from the Standard Plastic Catalog, 1966.

MATTEL TOYS 1967

MATTEL, INC.
TOYMAKERS

SPACE
CRAWLER
5

REMOTE CONTROL FLEXIBLE
ARMS WITH GRASPING HANDS

PROTECTION FROM
HOSTILE ENVIRONMENT

ADAPTED FROM
OFFICIAL SPACE PROGRAM

Package size, 13" x 13" x 14"

NEW!

Major MATT MASON™ WITH MOON SUIT

#6303

**Major MATT MASON dons this special environmental
suit for all exploratory missions!**
Plastic MOON SUIT snaps over the astronaut (included) and
features attachable air pump for remote control arm movement.
Accessories include two-piece radiation detector, wrench,
screw driver, rock hammer and space labels.
Std. Pack: 6/12 Doz.   Wt: 5 Lbs.

PRINT   TV

NEW!
ROCKET LAUNCH PAK
#6305
Formidable defense weapon
against any odds! Includes
two-piece remote-control
rocket launcher with control
column and rocket that fires
caps (not included) in
immediate or in-flight action.
Plus ROTO-JET™ GUN, pair
of Walkie-Talkies, firing
string, safe knife, sheath,
belt and space labels.

NEW! MOON SUIT PAK
#6301
Essential equipment for
survival and space experi-
mentation! Includes molded
plastic moon suit with flexible
arms and grasping hand.
Air pump and tubing for
remote arm control, two-piece
radiation detector, interior
control console, screw driver
and rock hammer.

Individual punched blister card. 8½" x 12"

PREVIOUS PAGES AND ABOVE: The arrival of Major Matt Mason and a line of toys inspired
by the space program, from the Mattel Catalog, Fall 1967.

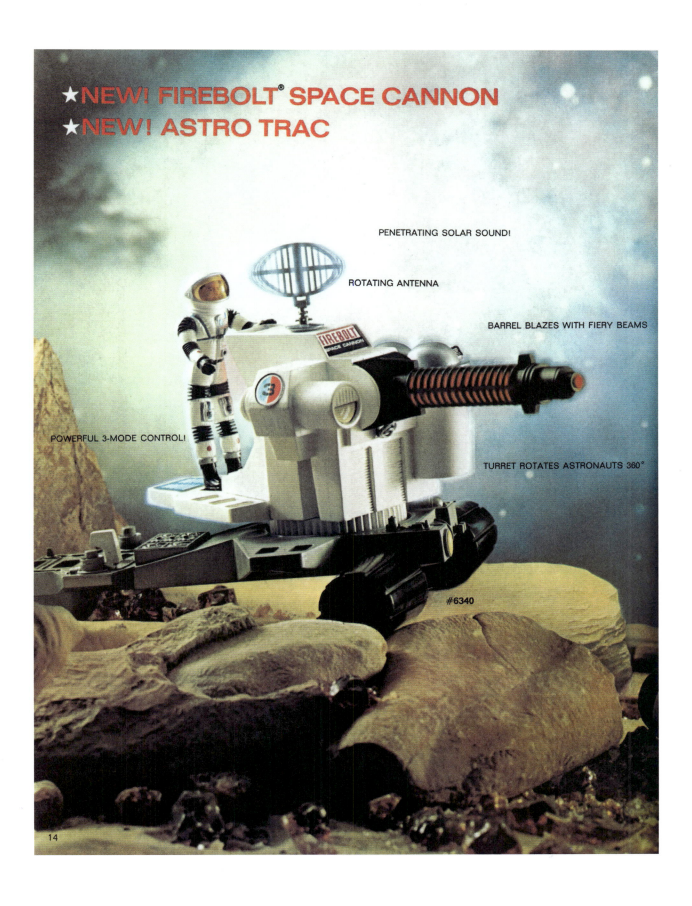

The Firebolt Cannon and Astro Trac, part of the Matt Mason line, from the Mattel Catalog, 1968.

U. S. Patent No. 3,010,252 and Other Patents Pending

915 FISHER · PRICE
Play Family
FARM

NEW Beautifully conceived in every detail of design and construction to fulfill a broad range of preschooler play-needs. The Big Red Barn and Silo hold a fascinating array of large scale farm figures and equipment, providing unlimited opportunities for creative self-expression "down on the farm" during the vital, early growth years. Unique features are the sculptured plastic animals with flexible, movable parts . . . and the barn door that opens with a "moo-ooo" sound! Silo has removable top, hayloft doors slide open, hinged carrying handle . . . finest wood and plastic throughout. An unsurpassed quality educational toy that develops imaginative and manipulative abilities for boys and girls 2 - 8.

CONTENTS: 11" x 8⅝" x 7" Barn, 10" x 5" Silo, 4-member Play Family, Horse, Cow, Lamb, Pig, Dog, Hen, Rooster, Tractor, Cart, Trough, 4-piece Fence.

PACKING: Each in box, ¼ doz. per 17 lb. shipper.

2

Our numerous and exclusive actions and designs are fully covered by patents and copyrights. Infringers, copyists and design pirates will be prosecuted to the full extent of the law.

©Fisher-Price Toys, Inc., 1967 and earlier. All Rights Reserved Under the International, Universal, and PanAmerican Copyright Conventions.

OPPOSITE: The Play Family Farm, from the Fisher-Price Catalog, 1968.
ABOVE: The Talking Tiles Learning Machine educational card game, from the Mattel Catalog, 1967.

NEW! THINGMAKER FEATURING FRiGHT FACTORY

#4522

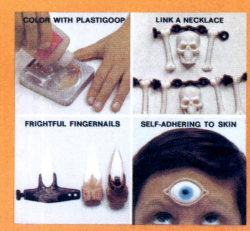

COLOR WITH PLASTIGOOP

LINK A NECKLACE

FRIGHTFUL FINGERNAILS

SELF-ADHERING TO SKIN

MAKE ALL KINDS OF FRIGHTFUL PLASTI-GRUESOME THINGS!

Be a customized creature from the fun-filled FRIGHT FACTORY with mirthful monster molds! Frighten with bloodshot eyes, scare with hairy shrunken heads and shock with fearful fangs! Form more fright-fun features like ghastly scars, monster-claw fingernails, bone necklaces, nosebones, skeletons, moustaches, lips, teeth and tongues. AUUGH! It's a Hollywood make-up man's dream! Contains metal THINGMAKER unit, seven different molds, PLASTIGOOP® (red, NITE-GLO, black and fleshtone), shrunken head mold core, blue and red beady eyes, hair, cooling tray, prying tool, handle, plastic knife, instructions, Styrofoam storage tray package.

Size 14⅝″ x 12⅝″ x 3-5/16″.
Std. Pack: 6/12 Doz. Wt: 25¼ Lbs.

The Thingmaker plastic molding machine, from the Mattel Catalog, 1967.

★NEW! tog'l™

Builds Action Toys

TOG'L, dynamic new way to make toys that move with blocks that move!

Each happy-colored TOG'L block features the Living Action Hinge that swings open — snaps shut — builds and bends! Children use built-in TOG'L versatility to put together real toys with real play value!

The five TOG'L sets progressively offer fun-to-build and fun-to-play pieces and parts for extra animation. TOG'L, Mattel's new dimension in creative play!

25

ABOVE: Tog'l, a building-block set, from the Mattel Catalog, 1968.
FOLLOWING PAGES: Bath-House Brass, a set of musical instruments inspired by plumbing fixtures, from the Mattel Catalog, 1968.

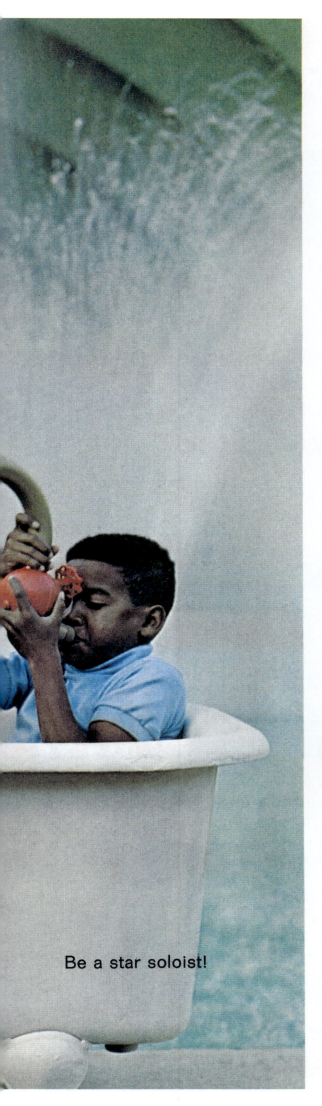

Be a star soloist!

World of
Musical Toys

★ **NEW! BATH-HOUSE BRASS**

Roaring, raucous BATH-HOUSE BRASS, hilarious-looking horns anybody can play just by humming!

Hum high or low, fast or slow! Be a parading TOOBA player — a Dixieland BRASSOON-IST — a musical FLOOGLEHORN genius! It's harmony in plumbing!

All BATH-HOUSE BRASS feature brass-plated plastic bells. pressure bulb with faucet handle and spigot mouth piece.

★ **NEW! FLOOGLEHORN #4901**
1 section, 10″ long.
Std. Pack: 1 Doz.   Wt: 16 Lbs.

★ **NEW! BRASSOON™ #4902**
2 sections, 15″ long.
Std. Pack: 6/12 Doz.   Wt: 11 Lbs.

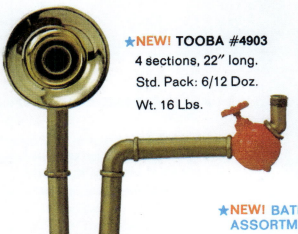

★ **NEW! TOOBA #4903**
4 sections, 22″ long.
Std. Pack: 6/12 Doz.
Wt. 16 Lbs.

Individual shrink-wrapped
pilferproof packages.

★ **NEW! BATH-HOUSE BRASS
ASSORTMENT #A4900**
Three unique BATH-HOUSE
BRASS instruments combined in one
assortment; 12 total.

6 ea. FLOOGLEHORN #4901
3 ea. BRASSOON #4902
3 ea. TOOBA #4903
FREE! FOUR-COLOR WINDOW BANNER
Std. Pack: 1 ea. (1 carton)   Wt: 22 Lbs.

HOT WHEELS, *fastest metal cars in the world!*

16 California custom miniatures 9 SPECTRAFLAME™ colors

Custom COUGAR —orange or blue

Custom MUSTANG —red or gold

Custom T-BIRD —aqua or gold

Custom FLEETSIDE —lavender or orange

DEORA —lime or gold

Custom BARRACUDA —aqua or lavender

Custom CAMARO —lime or blue

SILHOUETTE —lime or lavender

HOT HEAP™ —lime or orange

Custom EL DORADO —blue or gold

CHEETAH™ —orange or red

Custom VOLKSWAGEN —green or lavender

Custom CORVETTE —red or blue

Custom FIREBIRD —red or blue

FORD J-CAR —white

BEATNIK BANDIT™ —aqua or lime

Customized scale versions of stock cars, rods, racers!

HOT WHEELS/car specs

All HOT WHEELS have most of these features.
Side pipes
Power bulges
Raked body
Detailed undercarriage
Rear exhaust pipes
'Vinyl' tops
Contrasting interiors

Low-friction wheel bearings

Realistic 'mag' wheels — red-stripe racing slicks

Patented positive-action, torsion-bar suspension*
*Patent pending.

Movable hood — customized engine

Illustrated matching collector's button for every car

Punched-hole blister card, 5¾" x 6".

★ **NEW!** HOT WHEELS CAR ASSORTMENT NO. 1 #A6221
12 each of 8 metal cars, shown at the left, on set-up wire rack display with header card 96 total cars plus laminated Collector's Catalog.
Std. Pack: 1 ea. (1 carton) Wt. 16 Lbs.

★ **NEW!** HOT WHEELS CAR ASSORTMENT NO. 1 #A6231
Same contents as #A6221, without wire rack and Collector's Catalog.
Std. Pack: 1 ea. (1 carton) Wt. 13½ Lbs.

★ **NEW!** HOT WHEELS CAR ASSORTMENT NO. 2 #A6222
12 each of 8 metal cars, shown above, on set-up wire rack display with header card. 96 total cars.
Std. Pack: 1 ea. (1 carton) Wt. 16 Lbs.

★ **NEW!** HOT WHEELS CAR ASSORTMENT NO. 2 #A6232
Same contents as #A6222, without wire rack
Std. Pack: 1 ea. (1 carton) Wt. 7 Lbs.

2

3

★ NEW! STUNT ACTION SET

★ NEW! STRIP ACTION SET

Only HOT WHEELS™ defy gravity in the dare-devil loop! Hurl spectacularly, safely, over jump ramp, track gaps!

In, up and out of thrilling 360° loop

Incredible mid-air stunt leap

HOT WHEELS sprint down the straight-away! Sizzle over humps, race flat out for the finish! Make hills with pillows, boxes, books!

start a race anywhere... drop HOT WHEELS on the track and let 'em roll

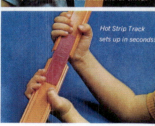

Hot Strip Track sets up in seconds!

STUNT ACTION SET #6201 /contents
1 HOT WHEELS Die-cast Metal Car with California Custom Styling
1 Matching Collector's Button
1 Dare-Devil Loop
2 Jump Ramps
16' of Hot Strip Track (8 sections)
1 HOT WHEELS International Collector's Catalog
1 Trestle
7 Joiners
1 Universal Clamp
Std. Pack: 6/12 Doz. Wt. 10¼ Lbs.

★ **NEW!** HOT WHEELS ACTION SET ASSORTMENT #A6203
Three sizzling HOT WHEELS Action Sets in single assortment. 12 sets total.
6 ea. HOT WHEELS STRIP ACTION SET #6200
3 ea. HOT WHEELS STUNT ACTION SET #6201
3 ea. HOT WHEELS DRAG RACE ACTION SET #6203
Std. Pack: 1 ea. (1 carton) Wt. 19 Lbs.

STRIP ACTION SET #6200 /contents
1 HOT WHEELS Die-cast Metal Car with California Custom Styling
1 Matching Collector's Button
10' of Hot Strip Track (5 sections)
5 Joiners
1 Universal Clamp
1 HOT WHEELS International Collector's Catalog
Std. Pack: 1 Doz. Wt. 12 Lbs.

More racing thrills with add-on accessories!
HOT WHEELS HOT STRIP TRACK PAK #6224
10' of action track for bigger, wilder layouts. 5 joiners.
HOT WHEELS FULL CURVE PAK #6225
Perfectly banked 180° curve!
HOT WHEELS DARE DEVIL LOOP PAK #6226
360° stunt loop.
HOT WHEELS HALF CURVE PAK #6227
Two 90° curves banked for blazing action!
Each in Std. Pack: 1 Doz. Wt. 6 Lbs.

★ **NEW!** HOT WHEELS ACTION ACCESSORY PAK ASSORTMENT #A6229
A two dozen assortment of ACTION ACCESSORY PAKS for the HOT WHEELS line.
8 ea. HOT WHEELS FULL CURVE PAK #6225
8 ea. HOT WHEELS DARE DEVIL LOOP PAK #6226
8 ea. HOT WHEELS HALF CURVE PAK #6227
Std. Pack: 1 ea. (1 carton) Wt. 12½ Lbs.

6

7

The first Hot Wheels cars and track sets, which made their debut in the Mattel Catalog, 1968.

The unmatched beauty of 16 customized collector's cars plus the accelerated excitement of high-speed racing!

Top-velocity HOT WHEELS are the custom class cars for collectors. With California custom stylings. Low-friction bearings. Exclusive torsion-bar suspension.* 'Mag' wheels. Red-stripe racing slicks. Dazzling SPECTRAFLAME paint jobs.

HOT WHEELS streak on race action sets that set-up in seconds — need no batteries or electrical current!

Curve for curve, action-laden HOT WHEELS out-race, out-stunt and out-distance every other metal miniature car on the track!

Car for car, the blazing vehicles include a half-dozen exclusive built-in features that start every miniature car collector clamoring for the entire HOT WHEELS line — all cars, all colors!

NEW!

DANCERINA

#3061

I dance real ballet steps!

She Toe-Dances perfectly!

Pirouettes beautifully!

Her head turns—stops and faces you—turns again as she spins!

DANCERINA dramatically performs authentic ballerina steps! She "bourees" daintily, toe-dancing forward or backwards. She whirls 'round and around to the left or right, "pirouetting" on either toe! She assumes the "passer le jambe" and many more classic poses! And most dramatically, DANCERINA "head spots" as she twirls! She turns her head, stops, then turns again like a real ballerina!

DANCERINA's sensational performance is a "dancer's secret!" Her magic tiara hides a control knob that directs each ballet step.

She's pure enchantment in a fluffy tutu, dancer's tights, and laced toe shoes! 33⅓ rpm ballet record, "The Song of the Flutes" from *The Nutcracker Suite*, is included.

She "toe-dances" . . .

"Pirouettes" . . .

Bows gracefully!

Tiara control—Just push in . . . or turn.

package showcases DANCERINA action photo.

24" DANCERINA action doll with rooted ponytail hairdo and removable costume is battery-operated. Batteries not included.

Std. Pack: ½ Doz.
Wt: 30 Lbs.

13

Barbie Christie Stacey & JULIA

Look who's talking! H-style dolls now broadcast fashion secrets!

Talking CHRISTIE™ #1126

Sweet-talking *CHRISTIE* would "like to be a fashion model!" Says more phrases, too! Pretty teen shows off yarn-trimmed bathing outfit. Luxurious eyelashes and rooted hair style.

Talking STACEY™ #1125

BARBIE's British chum! She talks with a delightful English accent! Real eyelashes, bendable poseable legs, 2 hair colors.

NEW!

Talking JULIA #11

TV Success Story

Television's fabulous "Julia" makes her fashion doll debut... speaking in Diahann Carroll's lovely voice! Wins admiring glances with glittering culottes and Diahann's own starry-eyed looks! Flirty eyelashes, lifelike bendable le

RECORDING

"What's playing at the cinema?"

"Let's go shopping with Barbie."

"I have a date tonight!"

"Hi, my name is JULIA

Talking BARBIE®

#11 5

Ever-popular *BARBIE* has lots to talk about and invites her friends to share in the fun 'n excitement of the grow -up world of fashion! Two-piece knit swim outfit real fashion eyelashes and choice of 3 hair colors. Bendable legs too!

Spanish-talking BARBIE

#834 3

Suggests "Vamos a los carnavales!" and many more phrases in lilting Spanish!

Talking units are operated by a tiny ring. No batteries necessary. Showcase package allows in-store talking demonstration. Each doll: 11¾" tall.

BARBIE, STACEY, CHRISTIE and JULIA are availa Std. Pack: 1 Doz.   Wt: 7½ Lbs.

SISTER SMALL-TALK®

#3011

Makes friends with "I like to play with you!" and more phrases in a lilting, easy-to-understand voice. Dashing hot-hued mini-dress with belt and vinyl boots. 10¾" tall.
Std. Pack: ½ Doz.
Wt: 6 Lbs.

BABY SMALL-TALK® #3010/3021

Perky *BABY SMALL-TALK* asks "Go bye-bye?" and says more sayings in a charming baby voice. Talking toddler features a kewpie-curl rooted hair-do, ribbon-and-lace trimmed dress with flower appliques. 10¾" tall.

Spanish-Speaking *BABY SMALL-TALK* #8360

"Tengo Hambre" says this small sweetheart as she recites 7 other phrases in fluent Spanish!
Std. Pack for either doll: 6/12 Doz.   Wt: 6 Lbs.

#3021

#3010/#8360

SMALL-TALK™ BEDDIE-BYE CASE

NEW!

#3004

Two-way tote carries *BABY SMALL-TALK*, *SISTER SMALL-TALK* or *BABY SMALL-WALK;* converts to bed, complete with decorative spread! Side pocket holds clothing.

Case size: 12"x5"x3".
Std. Pack: 1 Doz.
Wt: 11¼ Lbs.

MATTEL's SMALL ACTION DOLL ASSORTMENT

NEW!

#A3069

4 ea. *BABY SMALL-TALK* #3010

3 ea. *SISTER SMALL-TALK* #3011

5 ea. *BABY SMALL-WALK* #3027

Asst. Pack: 12 Items

Wt: 14 Lbs.

PREVIOUS PAGES: The first appearance of the Dancerina doll, from the Mattel Catalog, 1969.
OPPOSITE AND ABOVE: Talking dolls from the Mattel Catalog, Spring 1969.
FOLLOWING PAGES: Twiggy doll and fashion sets, from the Mattel Catalog, 1968.

Posies
2/6ᵈ

#1185   #1725   #1726

88

twiggy™

TWIGGY #1185

London's top teen model! Delicious in stripes and skinny mini-dress. Plus high, handsome boots and matching panties.
Twist 'N Turn waist, lifelike bendable legs, Twiggy hair-cut and real eyelashes. Clear posin' stand. 11" tall.

Std. Pack: 1 Doz.
Wt: 7¾ Lbs.

See-through package with free autographed picture!

★ **NEW! TWIGGY ENSEMBLE PAK COSTUMES**

FRANCIE® and CASEY® wear all costumes made for **TWIGGY**
NEW! TWIGGY-DO'S #1725
Striped knit reaches new rave-length! Purse, double-strand necklace, socks.

NEW! TWIGGY TURNOUTS #1726
Metallic mini-dress plus striped two-piece swimsuit!

NEW! TWIGSTER #1727
Anywherewear as checks and stripes knit together! Fringed scarf, complete make-up kit!

NEW! TWIGGY GEAR #1728
Vinyl jump suit belted and bloused in knit! Hat 'n camera.

Hangers and footwear included.
Each in Std. Pack: 1 Doz.   Wt: 3½ Lbs.

★ **NEW! TWIGGY ENSEMBLE PAK ASSORTMENT #A1388**
Six each of four costumes; 24 total in display shipper.
Std. Pack: 1 ea. (1 carton)
Wt: 8 Lbs.

#1727   #1728

89

"TWIGGY" ©1967 Minnow Co., Ltd. and Twiggy Enterprises Ltd.

More new
HOT WHEELS
cars !
The action
starts here.

Hot Wheels cars, from the Mattel Catalog, 1969.

SUPER-EYES!™

60

The Super-Eyes set, which could be adapted into a microscope, periscope, or telescope, from the Mattel Catalog, 1969.

"*I Have the* **Power!**"

He-Man, *Masters of the Universe,* 1983

CHAPTER THREE

Tapping into Technology

Mattel was on top of the world at the dawn of the 1970s, but the top came with its own unique set of challenges. The next fifteen years would see Mattel take big risks, ride out failures, and adapt to ultimately become a stronger company. It would also see Mattel begin a long tradition of giving back through the Mattel Children's Foundation, which was founded in 1978 to make a difference in the lives of children and families around the world.

Within twenty years, Mattel had grown from a small mom and pop shop into a Fortune 500 Company. They struggled at times to keep pace with that growth, moving buildings multiple times and hiring people faster and faster.

1970–1985

Happy 16th Birthday BARBIE

SPRING INTRODUCTIONS
MATTEL TOYS '74

MATTEL

Toys'71

PRE-SCHOOL TOYS

Mattel Movin' Ahead 1980

MATTEL TOYS 1980

MATTEL
TOYS 1970

OUR TWENTY-FIFTH YEAR

HOT WHEELS Club   Collectors' Edition 50¢

HOT WHEELS RACING WORLD

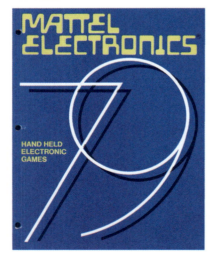

MATTEL ELECTRONICS
79

HAND HELD ELECTRONIC GAMES

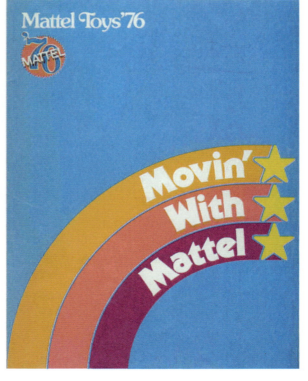

Mattel Toys'76

MATTEL

Movin' With Mattel ★ ★ ★

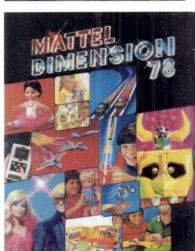

MATTEL DIMENSION '78

There hadn't ever been time to restructure the way business was done; and then, in 1970, Ruth was diagnosed with breast cancer. Ruth wrote in her autobiography, *Dream Doll*, that after taking time off for treatment and a mastectomy, "I was never able to grab hold of things at Mattel and regain control." Ruth and Elliot exited Mattel in 1974, ready for a respite, and, in Ruth's case, ready for a change. Ruth went on to found a new company which created and sold the first ever prosthetic breasts for women who had undergone mastectomies.

Throughout the early 1970s, Mattel continued to innovate even as the company raced to maintain their rapidly growing infrastructure and operations. They created a line of Tuff Stuff pre-school toys that had a then unheard of 5-year warranty and was very popular with parents, and Baby Tender Love, a deluxe baby doll with playsets and outfits sold separately. They also developed more action figures for boys, including Big Jim and Pulsar, and continued to add electronic and talking elements into board games.

In 1977, Mattel Electronics released handheld football and racing video games. Those sold well enough that they released the very first Mattel video game console, the Intellivision, in 1979. Within five years, Mattel had sold over three million consoles, capturing almost 20% of the American market. However, unlike other toy lines, the video game market fluctuated unpredictably, and consoles and games were very costly to develop, test, and market. In 1983, Mattel took a $283 million loss on video games, almost bankrupting the company.

Luckily, venture capital provided a new infusion of cash, allowing Mattel time to right the ship. They sold off Mattel Electronics and other loss leaders and focused on what had always made Mattel stand out: a commitment to well-crafted, affordable, imaginative toys that brought joy to kids.

With that overarching principle in mind, Mattel redoubled their efforts with Barbie, introducing bigger and better Dreamhouses, playsets, pets, cars, and so many fashions. It was important to the Mattel team that Barbie keep moving forward, and they made a point to take inspiration from the cultural trends of the time. In 1980, Mattel debuted the first Black Barbie doll, designed by Kitty Black Perkins, and decked out in a sparkly red jumpsuit with a disco skirt. In 1985, Mattel debuted a new ad campaign for Barbie with the slogan "We Girls Can Do Anything." Barbie had always provided girls a way to sample all of those mysterious grown-up moments by playing out parties, dating, weddings, and careers. But Mattel wanted to inspire girls to think broader. More and more women were entering the workforce and securing bigger and better jobs, and Mattel believed Barbie's world should reflect this shift. Options like Day-to-Night Barbie and even a Barbie Home and Office playset allowed girls to imagine what a corporate life could look like.

With Barbie still such a strong seller, Mattel hoped to land a similar foothold with boys in the action figure space. The Masters of the Universe action figures and playsets debuted in 1982, led by muscle-bound He-Man. He and his extraterrestrial friends and foes from the planet Eternia captured boys' imaginations all over the world. Mattel partnered with Filmation to produce a cartoon series, *He-Man and the Masters of the Universe*, which premiered in 1983, further boosting demand for all things He-Man.

By 1984, Masters of the Universe reached $350 million in sales. Later that year, the Masters of the Universe series culminated with an animated movie titled *The Secret of the Sword*, which introduced a new spinoff cartoon series for girls, *She-Ra: Princess of Power*. Of course, Mattel was ready for their newest action figure offering to hit big, and released a line of She-Ra toys for girls, including She-Ra's Crystal Castle.

Mattel had found its footing again, and the future was looking brighter than ever.

OPPOSITE, CLOCKWISE FROM UPPER LEFT: Mattel catalog covers from 1974, 1971, 1970, 1971, 1978, 1976, and 1979, and 1980.

Catalog Archive

Brain Drains game, from the Mattel Games Catalog, Spring 1970.

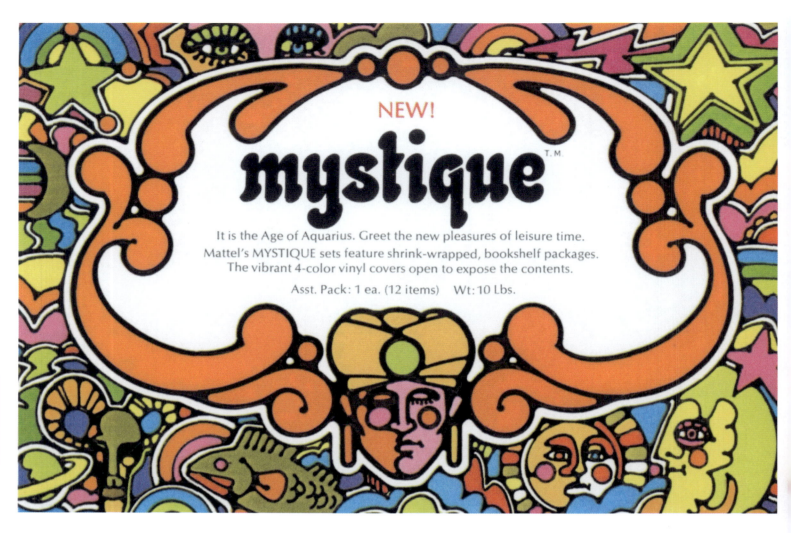

NEW!
mystique™·

It is the Age of Aquarius. Greet the new pleasures of leisure time.
Mattel's MYSTIQUE sets feature shrink-wrapped, bookshelf packages.
The vibrant 4-color vinyl covers open to expose the contents.

Asst. Pack: 1 ea. (12 items)   Wt: 10 Lbs.

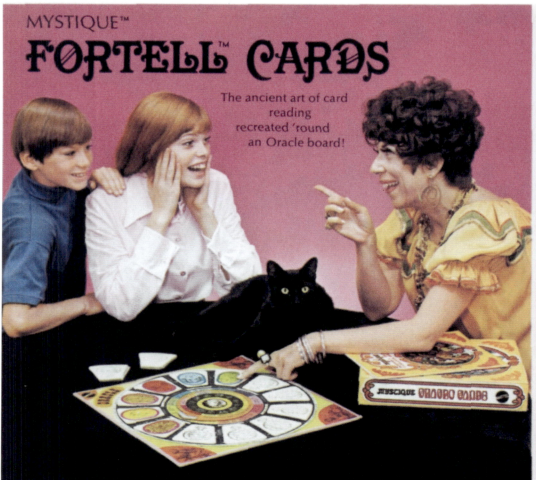

MYSTIQUE™
FORTELL™ CARDS

The ancient art of card
reading
recreated 'round
an Oracle board!

NEW! MYSTIQUE™ FORTELL CARDS #5475

Uniquely-created tarot cards are drawn and revealed in solitaire or groups. Each time, there are new discoveries, tantalizing predictions.

Complete with 48 Fortell Cards, folding board, the Wheel of the Zodiac and instructions.

Std. Pack: ⅓ Doz.   Wt: 5 lbs.

ABOVE: Mystique and Fortell Cards, from the Mattel Games Catalog, Spring 1970. OPPOSITE: The Wizzzer spinning top toy, from the Mattel Catalog, Spring 1970.

NEW!

BABY WALK'N PLAY

I bounce my yo-yo!
I paddle my ball
all around!

Come play with me!

All-activity toddler—features 4 exciting
actions—she plays paddle ball—
bounces her yo-yo—waves her hanky
and then walks all by herself. Miniature
doll moves both arms but concentrates
action in her right one—moving up
and down vertically. Just attach
accessories to make her play.

11" tall with rooted hair, polka-
dot dress. Battery-operated; all
toys pictured are included.

Std. Pack: ½ Doz.   Wt: 9 Lbs.

OPPOSITE: Living Barbie, from the Mattel Dolls Catalog, Spring 1970.
ABOVE: Baby Walk 'n' Play, a doll with movement technology, from the Mattel Dolls Catalog, Spring 1970.
FOLLOWING PAGES: Six new games from the Mattel Games Toy Fair Catalog, 1970.

BiG THUMB #5404

Thumb people play for whopping good fun. BIG THUMB grabs the chips—the hammer whops 'n wallops him before he steals them all! Thumbtimes win . . . thumbtimes lose! Always thumb fun!

Playing pieces:
1 BIG THUMB
3 Soft, Plastic HAMMERS
1 4-color Game Cloak
20 Chips
Std. Pack: 1 Doz.   Wt: 18 Lbs.

Bandersnatch #5434

Pass the cards—grab the spinner! Build the goofy-looking Bandersnatch—Be first—you're the winner!

Playing pieces:
4 Bandersnatch bodies (with noses, feet and tails)
4 Spinners
16 Cards
Std. Pack: ½ Doz.   Wt: 10 Lbs.

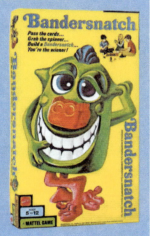

SHOO FLY PIE #5448

Hi, Man! Meet our pie man! Shoo the fly off his pie! Wiggle . . . wobble . . . no hands allowed. It's cherry pickin' fun.

Playing pieces:
1 Cherry Pie, 12" Round
1 Pieman Base
12 Plastic, Hole-punched Cherries
3 Support Rods
2 Connectors
24 Straws
Std. Pack: ½ Doz.   Wt: 9 Lbs.

frenzy

by Mattel

Whop! Can you stop BIG THUMB?
Zing! SPRING CHICKEN'S on the wing!

 **#5401**   Fingerdinger Man races any finger while you race the Slowman! Hit the panic button first and beat Fingerdinger Man for finger flinging fun!   Hooray Fast Kid!

Playing pieces:
1 Fingerdinger Man
1 Slowman
1 Ramp with automatic Dinger Button
2 Panic Button pads
Plus cards, labels, elastic bands and instructions.

Std. Pack: 1 Doz.
Wt: 16 Lbs.

 **#5449**

Spin marble eggs 'round the nest.
Put 'em on a feather or two.
Be careful, SPRING CHICKEN has a surprise for you!

Playing pieces:
 1 SPRING CHICKEN
   (head and snap-on neck)
 1 Spring
 1 3-Dimensional Nest
 4 Feathers with Die-Cut
   Slot
50 Marble Eggs
   Std. Pack: 1 Doz.
   Wt: 19 Lbs.

 **WIPE-OUT RACE GAME** #5439

You choose your speed, pick the pace . . . and win race! Includes 4 'gear' boxes, *HOT WHEELS* spinner, fold-out track plus all playing pieces. For 2 to 4 *HOT WHEELS* fans.

Std. Pack: ½ Doz.   Wt: 12 Lbs.

Sizzlers

Race 'em. Charge 'em. Run lap after lap at super speeds. Re-charge again and again for instant power.

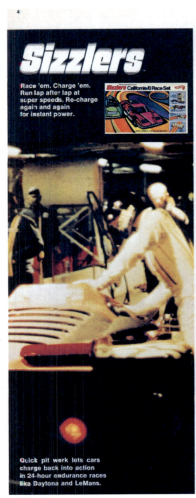

Quick pit work lets cars charge back into action in 24-hour endurance races like Daytona and LeMans.

START GATE/Cars scorch away in side-by-side start.

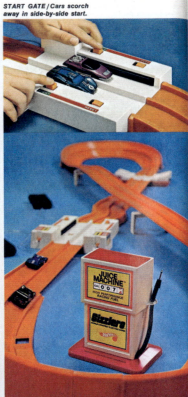

JUICE MACHINE™/portable recharge power from two or four "D" batteries.

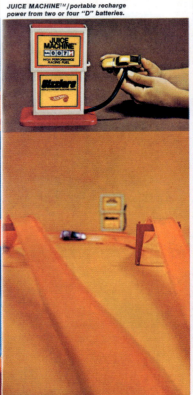

SPEEDOMETER/automatically clocks high speed runs.

8 CALIFORNIA/8™

Two SIZZLERS™ cars challenge a figure 8 course, "refuel" at the JUICE MACHINE™ then blaze off through the Dual—Lane SPEED BRAKE™ and Esses. Dual-lane Lap Counter records every circuit of the two dual lane curves and 28 feet of track.

0 LAGUNA OVAL™

Race your SIZZLERS™ cars around the big Indy-style oval. Recharge at the Juice Machine™ and you're ready for more fast laps around the 16 feet of track and two full curves. Joiners and trestles come with sets.

8 NEWPORT PACER™

Blaze your SIZZLERS™ cars around this high bank oval. Brake down for the tricky esses, then go all out through the speedometer. One trip to the Juice Machine supplies power for lots of laps around the two full curves and 14 feet of track.

---

from Speed Shift to Stop Pop!

HOT WHEELS® action lets you scorch off like a real hotshoe when you speed shift to racing speeds . . . watch while your drag chute blossoms at the end of the strip after a winning run . . . put on a thrill show with all the loops, jumps and spills of big time stunt driving and flying.

1 DRAG 'CHUTE™ Stunt Set . . . defy gravity in the loop-the-loop, soar across space then snap to a chute-popping stop.

2 Sky Show Set . . . the AERO LAUNCHER™ races down track and catapults stunt plane into the air. Six planes perform loops, rolls or sprints.

3 Dual-Lane ROD RUNNER™ . . . control the "go" with this power booster. Set the speed control, push speed shift stick down when your car goes through the Rod Runner.

4 Single-Lane ROD RUNNER™ . . . truly explosive acceleration for single track setups.

21

Pages from the Mattel Hot Wheels Collector Club Catalog, 1970.

Design your own road race course
with HOT WHEELS® accessories.

There's a lot of racing fun in putting
together a big competition course. Join sets
and accessories with your friends for super
speedways that fill the backyard. Do you
want a fast track or a difficult one? HOT
WHEELS® exciting accessories let you build
your very own test of your driving skill.

1|2|3go

1 Bridge Pak
2 Full Curve Pak
3 Trestle Pak
4 Dare-Devil Loop Pak
5 Dual-Lane Curve Pak
6 Hot Strip Track Super Pak
7 Jump Ramp Pak
8 Competition Pak
9 Dual-Lane ROD RUNNER™
10 Dual-Lane Speedometer
11 Dual-Lane Lap Counter
12 Collectors Cases, 12-24-48 car
Rally Cases, 12 and 24 car

An exciting
blend of traditional
classic and old-
world designs and
distinctive new
models debut
for 1970.
Designers give
each car its
individual
HOT WHEELS
personality.

1 EVIL WEEVIL™ Meanest bug that ever roared
2 HAIRY HAULER™ Wedge-nosed pick-up and power
3 COCKNEY CAB™ London's foggy fast one
4 CLASSIC CORD The Classic of Yesterday and Today
5 AMX/2 American Motors' Italian built bomber
6 OLDS 442 Detroit's 1970 super stocker
7 SUGAR CADDY™ High speed and high style
8 GRASS HOPPER™ Four wheel drive for off-road roaming

OFFICIAL
HOT WHEELS®
CLUB MEMBERSH
AWARDED TO

Joey Alpern

1970-1971

First showi of the new
CORD

the
CLASSIC
and the
NEWCOMERS

6037 Snake & Mongoose Drag Set

All the excitement of Real Drag racing with this set. The "Christmas Tree" start prepares the racers through a series of orange "lights". The Green lets them GO! If they go before the green they'll get a RED to disqualify. The BIG BELTER sends the cars screaming down the track and the finish gate indicates the winner.

Contains: Big Belter with match maker: 32 ft of Hot Strip Track, 16 joiners: 2 chute traps: 2 parachutes: finish gate and Mongoose Drag Racing Cars.

8618 Drag Chutes

available seperately

Converts existing sets to Drag Racing sets. Cars actually pick-up chutes to slow them before the end of the track! Chute appears to "pop" from the rear of car.

Contains: 2 chute traps: 2 Parachutes; complete with hooks.

ZAPPIT™ PAK #5824

High-speed pocket booster and HOT WHEELS® car! For off-track action wherever you go! Race on HOT WHEELS® track, too! Fold up and fit in a pocket! Snap together, add starter! It's ready!

Std. Pak: 48   Wt: 27 Lbs.

BUG BITE™ Set #5645

An aim-to-win game of skill!
Roll down the track . . . try to stop on highest score—WITHOUT getting gobbled up by Hungry Bug!

The Set:
1 HOT WHEELS® car
1 Hungry Bug with snap-shut mouth trap
7 feet HOT WHEELS® track
7 Joiners
Number labels

Std. Pak: 12
Wt: 5.8 Lbs.

SNAKE BITE™ Set #6692

The Set:
2 HOT WHEELS® cars
1 Snake with snap-shut jaws
14 feet HOT WHEELS® track
4 HIGHWINDER™ Sections
1 Printed full color board base
2 ZAPPIT™ boosters
13 Joiners
1 each catalog, Instruction Sheet and Warranty Card

Std. Pak: 6   Wt: 9 Lbs.

Race up, around 'n down to the finish!

Winner escapes— loser gets the Snake Bite!™

9

OPPOSITE: The Snake and Mongoose Drag Set, from the Mattel Catalog, 1972.
ABOVE: The Hot Wheels Zappit, Bug Bite, and Snake Bite sets, from the Mattel Toys and Hobbies Catalog, 1972.

GLIDERS #5493

Is it a bird? Is it a plane? It's one of Mattel's 4-glider models. All with 3-D design. So they look and feel real. And fly well out-of-doors no matter what weather conditions prevail.

For serious missions or stunt happy fun you'll have a good flight with one of these gliders.

Std. Pack: 24 Wt: 14 lbs.

PROPS #5496

For ace cub pilots, 3-dimensional prop planes that you wind up with a revolutionary zip cord. Then up-up and away, into the wild blue yonder.

For serious flying missions or high stunting fun. In 2 designs that look and feel real. And with a wing span of 20″ and fuselage of 15″, you'll be flying high no matter what weather conditions prevail.

Std. Pack: 12 Wt: 18 lbs.

ABOVE: Sky Riders glider and propellor planes, from the Mattel Games, Crafts, and Hobbies Catalog, 1971.
OPPOSITE: Live Drive, a driving simulator with interchangeable illustrated "windshields" for traveling by road, water, air, or space, from the Mattel Pre-School Catalog, 1971.

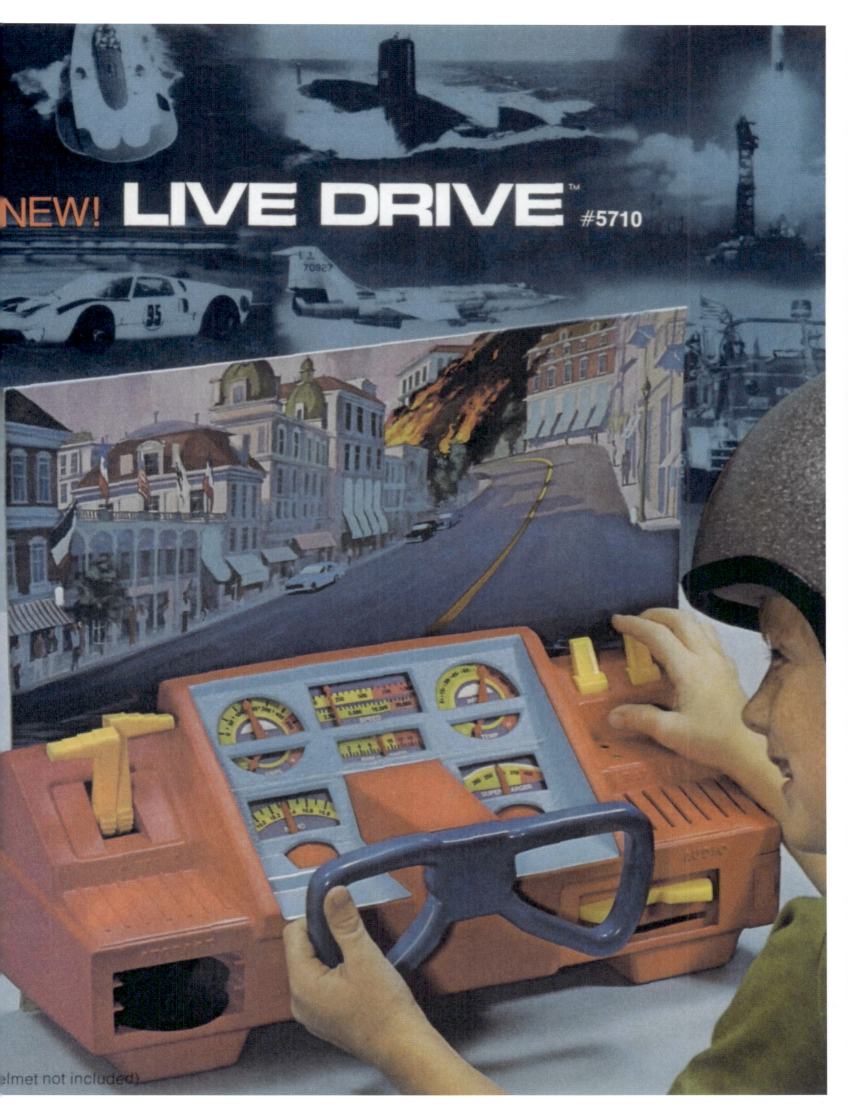

NEW! **LIVE DRIVE**™ #5710

(Helmet not included)

ZZZOOM·IT

INSIDE
OUTSIDE

IN SPACE
ANY PLACE!

AT DOORS
OFF FLOORS

THE SUN SET™ TODAY'S TOGETHER TEENS!

Golden tan outdoor beauties who chase the sun... From the lush Hawaiian surf to the playful sands at Lauderdale! The gals have long blonde hair, Twist 'n Turn waist and bendable legs. Personal beach towel, and Sunglasses. Ken has bendable legs and beach towel, too. The Sun Set is really the sunrise in BARBIE'S® World.

Malibu SKIPPER®
#1069

Malibu
BARBIE®
#1067

NEW! Malibu KEN®
#1088

Malibu FRANCIE®
#1068

Malibu SKIPPER®

Lithe bikini-clad beachcomber who likes to make dreamy sand castles. Beach towel, sunglasses. 9½" tall.
Std. Pack: 12   Wt: 10 Lbs.

Malibu BARBIE®

BARBIE digs the California coast, especially the fun at Malibu! Nifty one-piece swimsuit plus beach towel and sunglasses. 11½" tall.
Std. Pack: 12   Wt: 10½ Lbs.

NEW! Malibu KEN®

KEN is in the swim with the tan to prove it. Beach towel. 12" tall.
Std. Pack: 12   Wt: 11 Lbs.

Malibu FRANCIE®

A cheery personality as warm as the sun! FRANCIE shines in her tank-top swim gear. Beach towel and sunglasses. 11" tall.
Std. Pack: 12   Wt: 10½ Lbs.

THE SUN SET featured in its own 4-color packaging. Look for them in the World of Barbie® Center.

PREVIOUS PAGES: The Zzzoom-It, a frisbee disc slingshot toy rebranded in 1976 as the Super Shooter, from the Mattel Catalog, 1971.
ABOVE: The introduction of Malibu Barbie, from the Mattel Dolls Catalog, 1971.

BARBIE 2-DOLL TRUNK #1004

10½″x13″x7″
Std. Pack: ½ Doz.
Wt: 18 Lbs.

BARBIE SINGLE DOLL CASE #1002

10½″x12½″x2⅞″
Std. Pack: 1 Doz.
Wt: 18 Lbs.

17¾″x13½″x3½″

BARBIE DOUBLE DOLL CASE #1007
Std. Pack: ½ Doz. Wt: 21¾ Lbs.

SKIPPER DOLL CASE #4966

10″x10″x2¾″
Std. Pack: 1 Doz.
Wt: 14 Lbs.

BALLET BOX #5023

10½″x10½″x3¾″
Std. Pack: 1 Doz.
Wt: 15 Lbs.

BARBIE HANGERS #1065

Perennial packet of dainty costume hangers.
Card: 10″x12¼″
Std. Pack: 2 Doz.
Wt: 4½ Lbs.

NEW! BARBIE'S® TOWN & COUNTRY™ MARKET
#4984

Open out realistic market and delicatessen where BARBIE® and her friends shop.

Action accessories include: Working shopping cart, check-out counter with actual moving check shelf, 3-D food and grocery packages, telephone, and a food/meat counter rack.

Dolls not included.
Std. Pack: 4 ea.
Wt: 17 Lbs.

NEW! BARBIE® COUNTRY CAMPER™ #4994

A way-out, up-to-date scene for BARBIE® and her pals. The camper is a great new accessory on wheels. Made of durable, washable vinyl plastic, complete with stick-on customizing decals. Scads of accessories include a pop-out tent, camping table with two camp chairs, luggage rack, and sleeping bags. Action features include slide out door, steering wheel, pop-up front window.

Std. Pack: 4 ea.   Wt: 16 Lbs.

Barbie's Town & Country Market, Country Camper, and accessories, from the Mattel Dolls Catalog, 1971.

NEW! Spin-Buggys™ *TOO WILD TO RIDE ON A TRACK!*

#4179 T-SQUARE™

#4178 PIT BOSS™

A brand new breed! Look at them zoom, listen to the engine roar—do spin-outs, turns, and wild, wild wheelies. Where do they get their go-power? WIZ-Z-ZER™ whirlers. Spin 'em. Set 'em in. They power the cars, make 'em race everyplace again and again. Except on track. SPIN-BUGGYS are too wild to ride on a track! California custom styling, highly detailed, with authentic racing labels plus actual engine noise.

#4178 PIT BOSS   #4179 T-SQUARE
Std. Pack: 12   Wt: 8½ Lbs.

**NEW! SPIN-BUGGYS™
DOUBLE DIG-OUT™ Set #4180**
Get: PIT BOSS™, T-SQUARE™, 2 whirlers, decals and dig-out rack.
Std. Pack: 12
Wt: 15 Lbs.

MATTEL

3

Spin Buggys, which used Wizzzers to make the cars move, from the Mattel Pre-School Catalog, 1971.

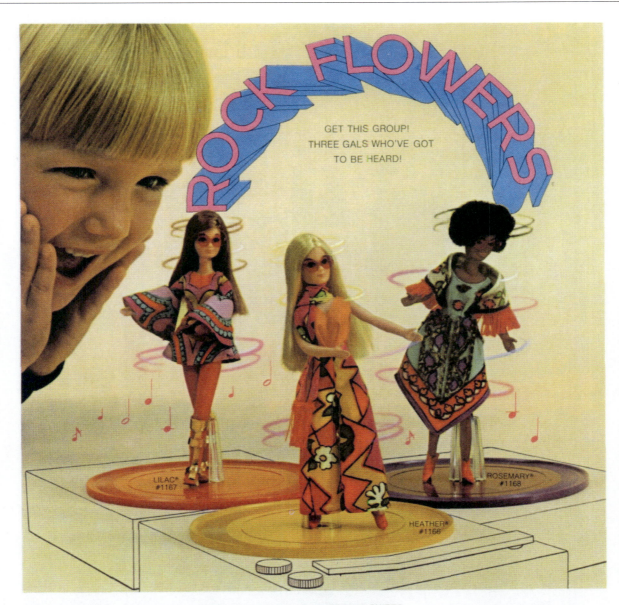

GET THIS GROUP!
THREE GALS WHO'VE GOT
TO BE HEARD!

LILAC®
#1167

HEATHER®
#1166

ROSEMARY®
#1168

Three hit personalities! Three great new records to go with them! Every ROCK FLOWERS has a brand new hit song written just for her! Plus the new ROCK FLOWERS group number on the flip side! Every ROCK FLOWERS has her own stand—fits right on her record! Pose her in any dancin' pose! Spin the record 'n watch her twirl. Far out fashion fun with a new dimension—music!

6½″ tall with rooted hair and eyelashes.
Open Window-Record-Flap   Attention-Getter Package stands on its own!
Std. Pack: 12   Wt: 9 Lbs.

Asst. #1169   24 pieces   Wt: 18 Lbs.
Asst. #1166   10 pieces   Wt: 7½ Lbs.
Asst. #1167   10 pieces   Wt: 7½ Lbs.
Asst. #1168   4 pieces   Wt: 3 Lbs.

Every ROCK FLOWERS
has her own package

24

ABOVE: Rock Flowers dolls, from the Mattel Dolls Catalog, 1971.
FOLLOWING PAGES: The live action Barbie and Ken range, from the Mattel Dolls Catalog, 1971.

A brand new kind of Live Action for this trio! Motorized stage with remote control — you set the tempo for any kind of dance, fast or slow! Dolls on stage come with a real 7″ two sided hit record, too, and BARBIE, KEN and P.J. each sing their own song. (Batteries not included.)

#1164 Live Action Dolls On Stage Sales Balanced Assortment

#1152, Live Action BARBIE On Stage — 8 each

#1153, Live Action P.J. On Stage — 4 each

#1153 Live Action P.J.®
On Stage
with play guitar
Std. Pack: 12 each
Wt: 18 Lbs.

Total: 12 pieces (1 each)
Wt: 18 Lbs.

#1152 Live Action BARBIE®On Stage
with play microphone for BARBIE.
Std. Pack: 12 each   Wt: 18 Lbs.

#1172 Live Action KEN® On S[...]
Std. Pack: 12 each   Wt: 19 Lb[...]

Live Action—
BARBIE®,
KEN® P.J.®,
and CHRISTIE®

BARBIE and her friends can rock to a swingin' backbeat or dance to prettier tempos! All the action's at your fingertips on the TOUCH 'N GO™ posin' stand.

Live Action BARBIE #1155
Std. Pack: 12   Wt: 10 Lbs.

Live Action KEN #1159
Std. Pack: 12   Wt: 10 Lbs.

Live Action P.J. #[...]
Std. Pack: 12 Wt: 10[...]

eal Action!
osin' like it is.

NEW! BARBIE® SUN 'N FUN BUGGY™ #1158

Motorized rocking seats!
Make BARBIE bounce and sway,
buggy can go in circles, too.

Use with *any* doll from
the World of BARBIE.®

(2 "D" batteries,
dolls not included.)

St. Pak: 12   Wt: 26½ Lbs.

Fun on wheels
for BARBIE® ar
and her friends.

NEW! BARBIE'S® Horse DANCER™ #1157

Make DANCER rear and race on
her Rocker Stand! Bend her legs
in lots of action poses!
Show her without the stand, too!
Sturdy Rocker Stand is operated
with hand control, makes hoof
beat sounds, too!

All of Mattel's Live Action and
Living Dolls (except KEN®) can
ride DANCER.

(Dolls not included.)

St. Pak: 12
Wt: 19 Lbs.

NEW! FASHION 'N SOUNDS™ for BARBIE®, P.J.® and CHRISTIE®

THE LATEST FASHION LOOKS STYLED TO GO WITH A SONG!

BARBIE'S® newest fashion
idea! Buy an outfit, get
a record with 2 hit
sides!

St. Pak: 12
Wt: 4 Lbs.

Live Action CHRISTIE® #1175
Std. Pack: 12   Wt: 10 Lbs.

COUNTRY MUSIC #1055   FESTIVAL FASHION #1056   GROOVIN' GAUCHOS #1057

NEW! FUTURE PHONE™ #4175

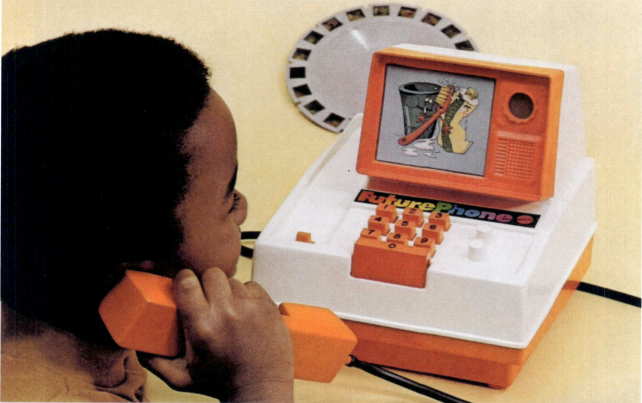

COLOR RECOGNITION   ODD JOBS   PHONICS & DICTION   PUSH BUTTON DIALING

40 SIGHT & SOUND CONVERSATIONS

The telephone of the future today. Voice comes from the receiver, with a bright projected picture, too.

Insert the record, select a friend and push the buttons.

The character appears on the screen and talks to the child about safety—"green means go, red & yellow mean stop"; manners—"If I gave you a cookie, you'd

say thank you"; good habits—"Do you brush your teeth?"; colors—"Reddy Red Fox, here, see my red fire engine."

40 different laugh and learn conversations on two program discs. Futuristic design—7¾" tall.

Std. Pack: 4   Wt: 10 Lbs.

ABOVE: The Future Phone, from the Mattel Pre-School Catalog, 1971.
OPPOSITE: Tuff Stuff made its debut alongside Mix 'n' Make building toys in the Mattel Dolls / Pre-School Catalog, 1972.

Dolls/Preschool
1972

Contents

Packed with each Mattel talking, walking or action toy or doll is a warranty registration card. It guarantees replacement or repair of any related mechanism within 90 days of purchase. Consumer claims are forwarded directly to Mattel.

All battery-operated products are offered without batteries. (Talking ring items do not need batteries.)

Dolls not included with ensemble pak costumes and assortments.

© 1972 Mattel, Inc., Hawthorne, California 90250. All Rights Reserved. Printed in U.S.A.

TUFF STUFF™

WITH THE 5 YEAR GUARANTEE!

GUARANTEED FOR 5 YEARS!
Any breaks or defects and your Tuff Stuff toy gets repaired, or you get a new one, or you get your money back! That's a pretty strong guarantee, but then, so are our Tuff Stuff toys!
Extended to original user only.

TUFF STUFF™ Numbers Truck #4754
This truck comes with a complete set of 10 Number Blocks. 'Cause it's rustproof, washable, colorfast, kids can use it for indoor, outdoor play. They just dump in the blocks to put them away! 5 Year Guarantee.
Std. Pack: 6   Wt: 13 Lbs.

TUFF STUFF™ ALPHA TRUCK™ #4755
This ride-on truck's packed with a set of 30 Alphabet Blocks. Kids can stack them in racks so they spell words down and across! ALPHA TRUCK is washable, rustproof, perfect for indoor, outdoor play. Has room underneath to tuck extra blocks away. 20" long, 10" tall. 5 Year Guarantee.
Std. Pack: 4   Wt: 29 Lbs.

TUFF STUFF™ Alphabet Blocks #4383
Thirty big, bright blocks made in letter shapes. A complete alphabet to help preschoolers learn plus 4 extra letters to help spell lots of words. Smooth, washable, stackable, they're also building toys for the very young. Sturdy plastic storage tub. 5 Year Guarantee.
Std. Pack: 6   Wt: 16 Lbs.

TUFF STUFF™ Number Blocks #6712
Zero to Nine two times, 20 big, bright number-shaped blocks give kids a lot to do! They can count up to 99, and beyond, if they're older or just stack and build if they're small. Smooth, washable, colorfast. 5 Year Guarantee.
Std. Pack: 6   Wt: 13 Lbs.

MIX 'N MAKE MOBILES™ #4773

First fitting fun for young ones! Parts and peg men come apart and interlock.
Std. Pack: 6
Wt: 7½ Lbs.

BUILDING TOYS
Favorite play shapes, but they are also ideal for first building efforts.

BUILD-A-TRAIN™ #4772
Std. Pack: 6
Wt: 6½ Lbs.

#4770 BUILD-A-TRACTOR™
Std. Pack: 12
Wt: 9 Lbs.

BUILD-A-SHIP™ #4771
Std. Pack: 12   Wt: 10½ Lbs.

MIX 'N MAKE ANIMALS™ #4777

More fitting fun in shapes kids love. Colorful parts interlock.

PICK-A-PATH™ #4774

Children can manipulate the beads through wooden blocks lots of different ways.

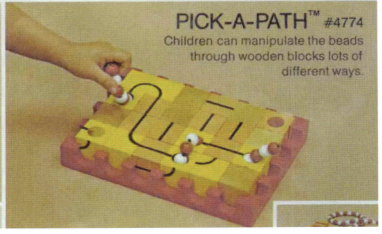

CRIB & PLAYPEN

Fisher-Price Toys run on child power.

Because when a toy is fueled by imagination it travels farther than anything.

The Jet that takes off from Play Family Airport lands on cloud cities.

And there's a musical Merry-Go-Round where no one ever asks for your ticket.

Our new Play Family Houseboat makes the bathtub a sea. With knees for islands.

And since child-power is half imagination, half pure energy, Fisher-Price puts in dozens of realistic details. Details that *do* things.

Look at our new Airport. With its own passenger jet, helicopter and a fleet of trucks and cars. The nozzle on the jet fueler fits every vehicle. The baggage rack can revolve. And the copter goes, "Whomp whomp." Children can appreciate that kind of thing.

So there they go. Into the air. Over the waves. Round and round in circles. That's child power.

©1972 Fisher-Price Toys, East Aurora, New York 14052
Division of The Quaker Oats Company

OPPOSITE: The Crib and Playpen range, from the Fisher-Price Catalog, 1972.
ABOVE: Fisher-Price advertisement, 1972.

BEANS FAMILY

A whole family of soft bodied dolls which can be flopped into thousands of amusing poses. Never have a family of dolls been so irresistible to children and adults alike. Soft tricot covered bodies are filled with Mattel's styrene "beans," which are completely safe and non toxic.

5244 Bedsie Beans

The "sleepy head" of the family.

5246 Bitty Beans

Beautifully Bashful.

5245 Booful Beans

With that "full of Mischief" look.

new!

5278 Talking Baby Beans

And now the chatterbox of the group who will express 8 cute phrases at random with a pull on her Chatty ring. Closed box packaging with soft full colour art.

The Beans Family dolls, from the Mattel Catalog, 1972.

ABOVE: Jack-in-the-Music Box, from the Mattel Catalog, 1972.
FOLLOWING PAGES: The Rumblers range of track-racing motorcycle toys, from the Mattel Catalog, 1972.

rRRumblers

The fastest wheels since Hot Wheels themselves. These detailed miniature die-cast Motorbikes and trikes are fun just to collect or Race on ANY miniature track system.

rRRumblers new!

6010 ROAD HOG   6011 HIGH TAILER   6031 MEAN MACHINE

6032 RIP SNORTER   6049 TORQUE CHOP   6048 3-SQUEALER

5947 Bold Eagle   5948 Choppin' Chariot   5949 Revolution

5883 ROAMIN' CANDLE

rRRumblers®

See the California Custom styling – chrome frames, pipes and Engines, Riders that can ride their machines in various stunt poses. Low-friction – high speed wheelbases all removable so that Rrrumblers can be played with separately. Blister packaged. Std. Pack 48 assorted.

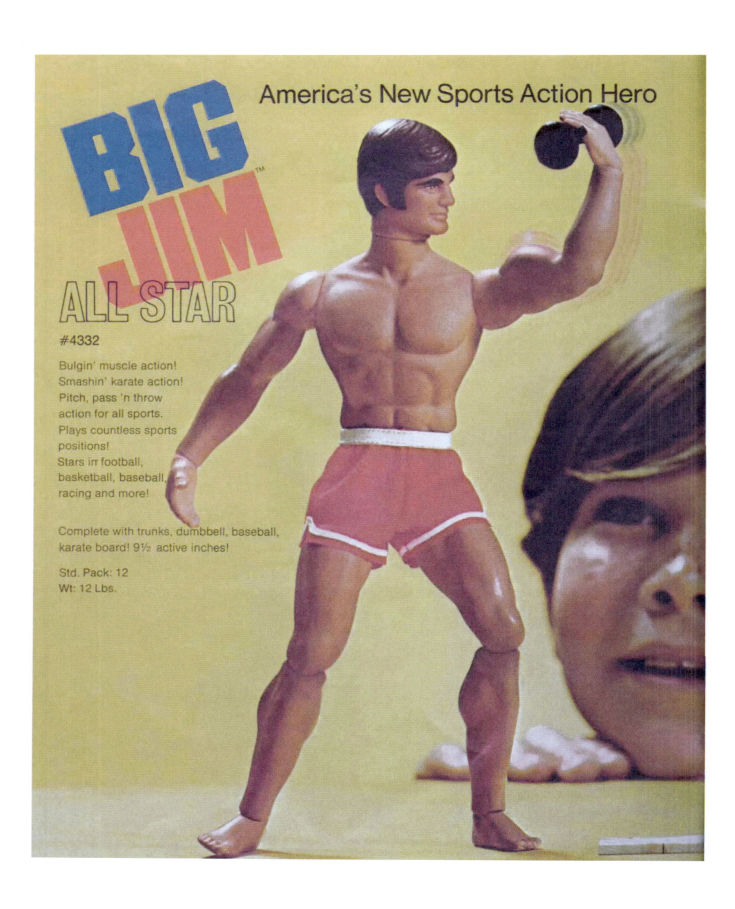

America's New Sports Action Hero

BIG JIM™
ALL STAR
#4332

Bulgin' muscle action!
Smashin' karate action!
Pitch, pass 'n throw
action for all sports.
Plays countless sports
positions!
Stars in football,
basketball, baseball,
racing and more!

Complete with trunks, dumbbell, baseball,
karate board! 9½ active inches!

Std. Pack: 12
Wt: 12 Lbs.

Big Jim made his debut in the Mattel Toys and Hobbies Catalog, 1972.

INSTANT REPLAY

RECORD PLAYER
WITH RECORDS
#5730

NEW! TWO-SIDED RECORDS!

A HOME RUN FOR MAYS

ANDRETTI WINS

NEW! TWO-SIDED RECORDS!

Collect 'em! Trade 'em! Hear about the Super Stars in baseball, basketball, football, hockey, racing, as they relive the action and excitement of their greatest days and plays! The tough INSTANT REPLAY record player is battery operated (one "D" cell), carrying size. Hear the action anytime, anywhere. It's easy to operate, too! The record pops in and plays. Just push a switch to pop it out or to hear it again. Each INSTANT REPLAY comes with 4, two-sided unbreakable records from the sports categories mentioned above. More exciting sports moments are available in separate 4-paks. There's a handy storage slot in every INSTANT REPLAY record player.
This set:
INSTANT REPLAY Unit
4 records

HEAR ALL THE BIG NAMES!

Willie Mays
Bart Starr
O. J. Simpson
Kareem Abdul Jabbar
Jerry West
and lots, lots more!

Al Kaline
Dick Butkus
Ernie Banks
Pete Maravich
Oscar Robertson

Std. Pack: 12   Wt: 8 Lbs.

Hear 2 Sides of Exciting Sports Action on Every INSTANT REPLAY™ Record!

New 2-sided records with Super Star picture on each side. Listen to a total of 66 seconds of sports action.
Collect and trade.
INSTANT REPLAY record 4-paks. Available in all of the following sports categories!

Std. Pack: 24
Wt: 3 Lbs.

Ice Hockey #5747

Basketball #5736

Sports Challenge #5735

Basketball #5739

Racing #5737

Football #5738

Baseball #5740

Football #5741

MATTEL

9

Instant Replay, a miniature record player which played recordings of commentary of memorable moments in sports, from the Mattel Toys and Hobbies Catalog, 1972.

64 Sling Shot Dragster 3 ins. 76 mm.
65 Saab Sonnet 2¾ ins. 73 mm.
66 "Mazda" RX 500 2⅞ ins. 73 mm.
67 Volkswagen 1600 TL 2¹¹⁄₁₆ ins. 68 mm.
68 Porsche 910 3 ins. 76 mm.
69 Rolls-Royce Coupe 3 ins. 77 mm.
70 Dodge Dragster 3 ins. 77 mm.
71 Jumbo Jet 2¾ ins. 69 mm.
72 Hovercraft SRN 6 3 ins. 76 mm.
73 Mercury Commuter 3 ins. 78 mm.
74 Toe Joe 3 ins. 76 mm.
75 Alfa Carabo 3 ins. 76 mm.

K22 Dodge Dragster 4½ ins. 115 mm.
K44 Bazooka 4⁷⁄₁₆ ins. 112 mm.
K39 Milligans Mill 4¼ ins. 108 mm.
K28 Drag Pack Mercury Commuter – Dragster & Trailer 9⅞ ins. 252 mm.

MATCHBOX Speed Kings

K36 Bandolero 4½ ins. 114 mm.
K30 Mercedes C111 4 ins. 102 mm.
K45 Maurauder 4⅛ ins. 105 mm.
K51 Barracuda 4¼ ins. 108 mm.
K40 Blaze Trailer 4 ins. 102 mm.
K42 Nissan 270X 4 ins. 102 mm.

MATCHBOX Speed Kings

The Matchbox Collector Catalog USA, 1973.

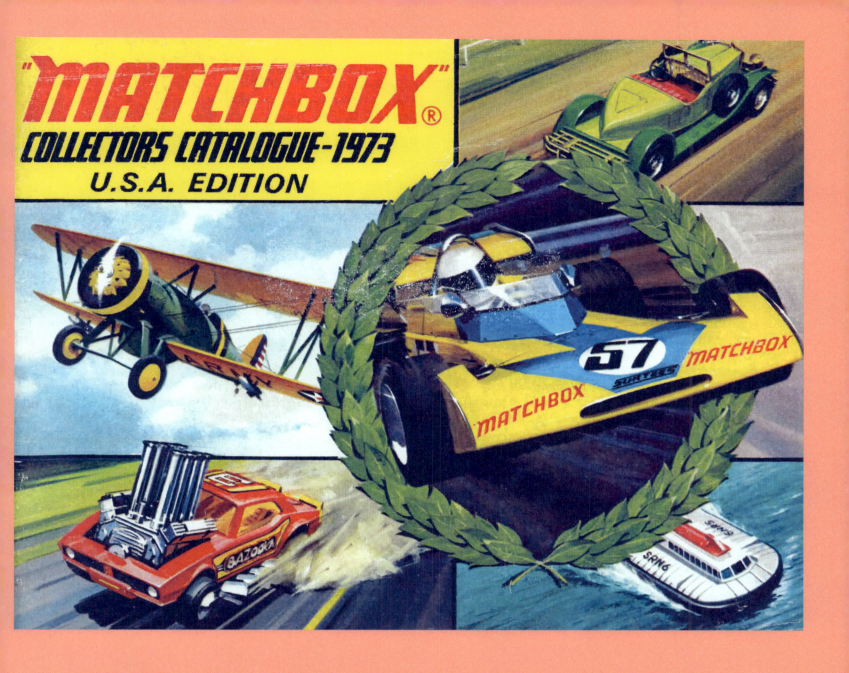

It was John William Odell, one of three partners in die-casting company Lesney Products, alongside Leslie Smith and Rodney Smith, who in 1952 would give Lesney the clarified direction and purpose it needed to succeed on a national and even global scale. John's daughter Annie's school had strict rules about what children could bring to school: only toys that fit inside of a matchbox were allowed. So that's exactly what John and Lesney decided to create: matchbox-sized car models.

By 1953, Lesney had a small line of Matchbox cars in stores. They kept the price quite low, and the cars quickly became popular buys for kids with limited pocket money. Over the next fifteen years, Lesney expanded considerably. At their largest, they employed several thousand workers—mostly women—in their factories in Hackney, East London. By 1969, they built more than 1,000 toy cars per minute.

Throughout the 1970s, the toy industry in the United Kingdom shifted significantly until a recession decimated local production. John and Leslie decided to retire in 1982 and sold Matchbox to Universal Toys, who in turn sold the brand to Tyco Toys a decade later. In 1997, Mattel purchased Tyco, and with that acquisition brought Matchbox into the Mattel family.

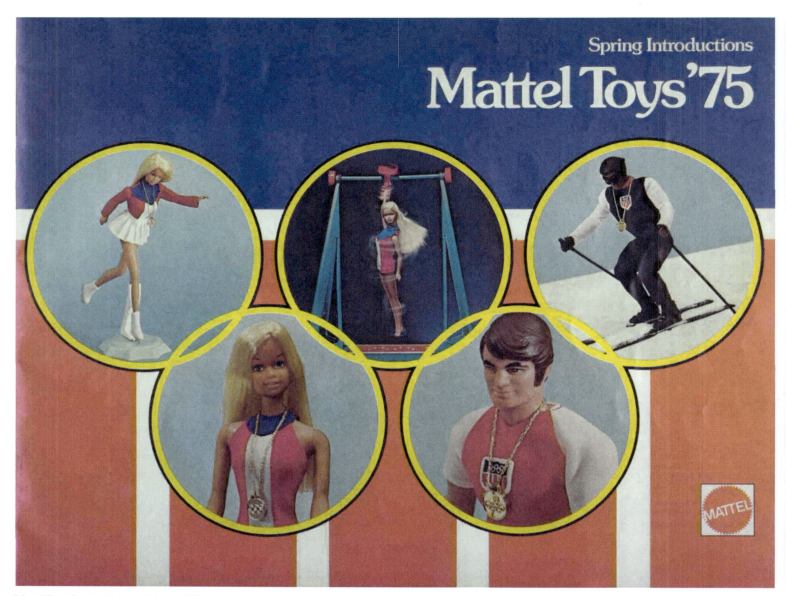

Mattel Toys Catalog Olympic Edition, 1975.

Gold Medal Big Jim, Mattel Toys Catalog Olympic Edition 1975

World of Big Jim, Mattel Toys Catalog 1973.

Big Jim Cycle Set, Mattel Toys Catalog 1973.

SPINWELDER

Take wild dragsters from design to finish with this amazing new welding toy! Spinwelder™ tool joins plastic parts together with localized friction heat. It's so easy! Touch spinning nib to plastic beam. The friction creates just enough harmless heat to join the two pieces.

If you change your mind about the finished design—pull pieces apart and start over. Repair breaks the same way. Or, if you LIKE IT, display it

as is, the joints are really tough! Set contains enough materials to make 2 super race vehicles. Use Spinwelder tool to rev 'em up then watch them drag over 60 feet. Operates on 6 volt lantern battery, not included. Contents: Spinwelder tool, 60 frame beams, 4 axles, panels, 6 fat wheels, 2 spoke wheels, 2 power wheel weights, decal set, 2 accessory sprues, 50 power tips, 4 traction bands, 1 rubberband, instructions.
#7331 Std. Pak 6/Wt. 21 lbs.

ZIZZORS

The fun electric scissors!

Zippity, snippity! It's fun and easy to create a whole paper world with these handy-dandy cordless, electric scissors! Safe—with guards for little fingers. Scissors come with twelve pop-out templates. Make houses, dolls, dogs, trees, an entire city and lots more. Children can choose any pretty colored paper they want. Fun for children 3-12. Paper and pencil not included. Operates on 2 "AA" batteries, not included.
#7908 Std. Pak 12/Wt. 6 lbs.

Spinwelder and Zizzors, Mattel Toys Catalog Flyer, 1974.

MATTEL Preschool
LI'L CAMPER™

BACK PACK with Tent 'n Tools
5-piece camping set really packs it in! Rugged pack comes with lots of room for gear. Pup-tent and poles detach easily from pack. Tent sets up to 38" x 25" x 18" big. Real canteen, play axe and shovel, too! All-weather durability. All washable.
#7052 Std. Pak 4/Wt. 15 lbs.

12

COOK STOVE
Super realistic cookout stove for camping out! Or for that great backyard adventure. Air pump makes water bubble to simulate boiling, forces air into pie and puffs it up. Bacon and egg even seems to fry! Looks like the real thing! Contents: Stove, skillet, fish, bacon, fried egg, pie, spatula.
#7064 Std. Pak 6/Wt. 21 lbs. 8 oz.

TRAIL BELT™
Rough 'n tumblers are all set to conquer the wilderness with this fully adjustable Trail Belt. It's lightweight and weatherproof with working compass, flashlight and whistle, and amply fillable canteen! Tough play axe and shovel are great for "cutting" through the underbrush. Flashlight operates on 2 "D" batteries, not included.
#7065 Std. Pak 6/Wt. 8 lbs.

13

Li'L Camper, Mattel Toys Catalog, 1974.

#7663 THUNDERSHIFT 500

ABOVE: The Thundershift racetrack, from the Mattel Catalog, 1975.
OPPOSITE: Flying Aces toy aircraft carrier set, from the Mattel Catalog, 1976.
FOLLOWING PAGES: The introduction of Mattel Electronics sports games, from the Mattel Catalog, 1977.

FLYING ACES™

ATTACK CARRIER™

"Pilots, man your planes! Captain to the bridge!" You're the task force commander! Signal the fleet by semaphore blinker! Launch 'em up, up & away! Attack Carrier is 3 feet long. Comes with Navy & Marine Flying Aces Corsairs, made of new TUFLITE™ material that's lightweight, flexible, safe—even indoors. Ship features a catapult launcher for one of the planes, while the other taxis into position for launching by remote control! Label set & instructions included. No batteries needed. Ship does not float. King-sized package has 4-color art.
9375 Std. Pak 6/Wt. 18 lb. 10 oz.

9375 ATTACK CARRIER Flag Ship
3 FEET LONG!

MATTEL ELECTRONICS™

AUTO RACE GAME

Mattel Electronics™ Auto Race game is self-contained! Needs no TV hook-up! Switch to start, the race is on! You steer, shift gears, avoid collisions & beat the clock! Driving action is simulated by moving light blips over 3 lanes. Player who completes 4 laps in the fastest time wins and hears the sound of victory! Auto Race game is portable. Weighs less than 5 ounces.

Game comes fully assembled with digital timer, built-in sound effects, precision lens, high-speed L.E.D. display, electronic printed circuit. Game is powered by 9-volt battery, not included. 90-day limited warranty and complete playing instruction included, plus game highlights on the product itself. Package has 4-color art.

#9879 Std. Pak 6/Wt. 4 lbs.

68

#9879 Auto Race Game

Self-contained, needs no TV set!

FOOTBALL GAME

Mattel Electronics™ Football game is self-contained! Needs no T.V. hook-up. It's the Big Game! The computer's on Defense! You're the ball carrier! Cut back! Speed up! Avoid tacklers! Run for daylight! Score a Touchdown! Hear the Victory "Charge"! Press the Play Status key for downs, yards-to-go, yardline. Press the Score key for the "score" and time remaining in quarter. And – when it's 4th and yardage you can try for a field goal or PUNT! Football game is portable. Comes fully assembled with built-in sound effects, precision lens, high-speed L.E.D. display, electronic printed circuit. Game is powered by 9-volt battery, not included. 90-day Limited Warranty and complete playing instructions included. Package is a "winner" with 4-color art all around.
#2024 Std. Pak 6/Wt. 4 lbs.

Self-contained, needs no T.V. set!
Field and Scoreboard light-up separately.

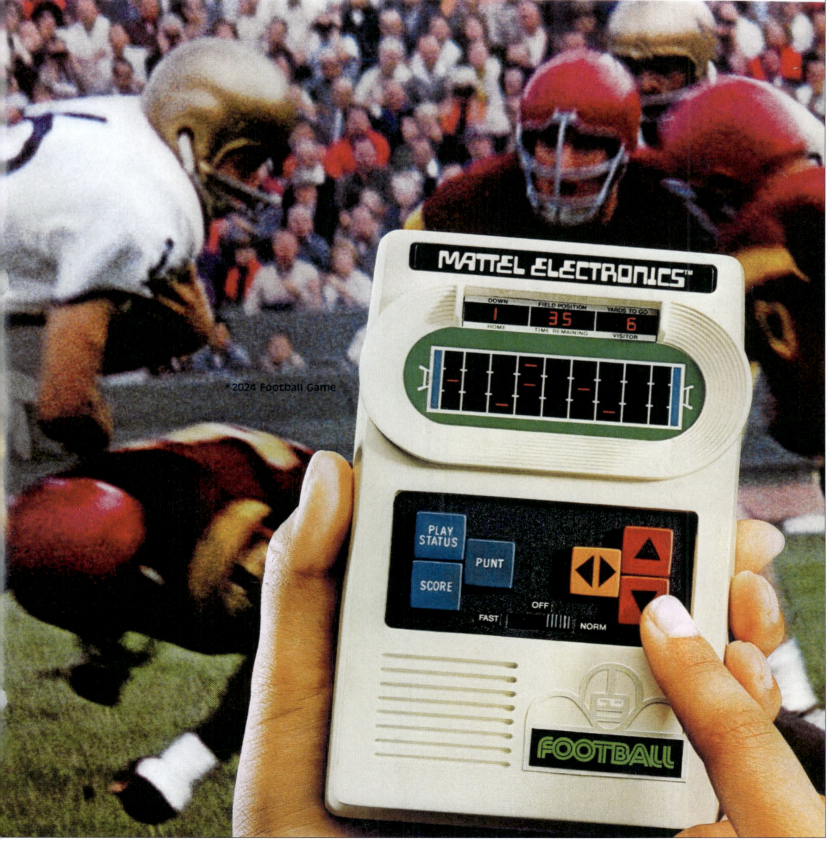

69

#2024 Football Game

Pages from the Mattel Living World Catalog, 1977–1978.

WOODTONE

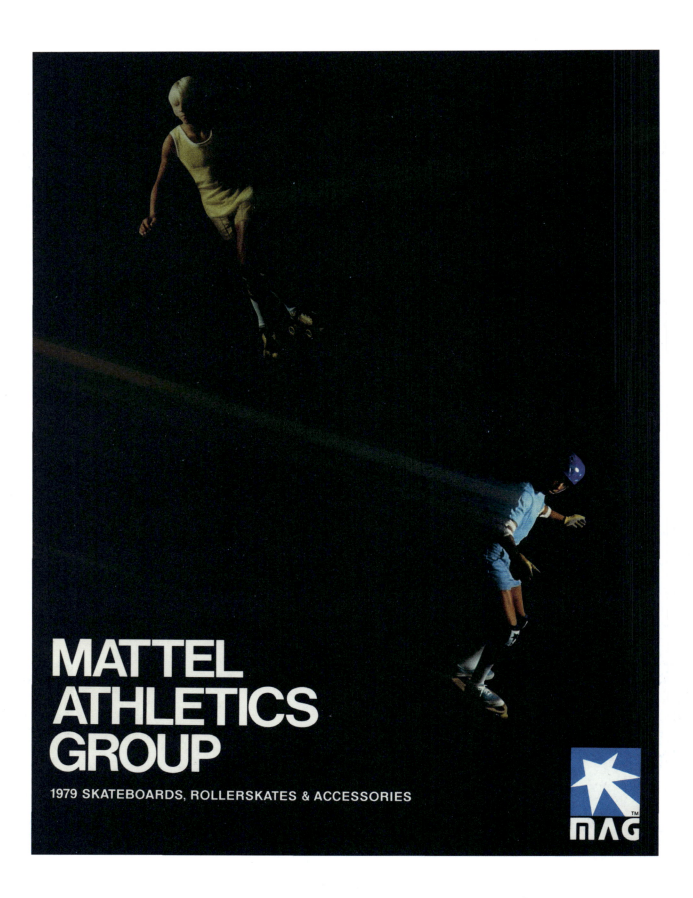

MATTEL
ATHLETICS
GROUP

1979 SKATEBOARDS, ROLLERSKATES & ACCESSORIES

MAG™

Cover and pages introducing skateboard and roller-skate ranges, from the Mattel Athletics Group Catalog, 1979.

Sunrunners™

All Sunrunners™ come equipped with:
- The exclusive M.A.G. wheel and truck system. (patents pending)
- Black oxidized steel chassis
- 5/16" tempered steel axles
- Poured urethane tires
- Precision bearings

SUPER PRO™
Stock No. 2889
Standard Pack: 6 pairs,
solid pk. or asst. sizes.
Weight/std. pk.: 36 lbs.
Available in 10 unisex sizes.
(See chart)

JUNIOR PRO™
Stock No. 1073
Standard Pack: 6 pairs,
solid pk. or asst. sizes.
Weight/std. pk.: 32 lbs.
Available in 7 unisex sizes.
(See chart)

SPORT PRO™
Stock No. 2888
Standard Pack: 6 pairs,
solid pk. or asst. sizes.
Weight/std. pk.: 34 lbs.
Available in 10 unisex sizes.
(See chart)

ALPHASKATE™
Stock No. 2890
Standard Pack: 6 pairs.
Weight/std. pk.: 28 lbs.
One adjustable size fits
shoe lengths 9" to 10" long.

UNISEX CONVERSION AND SIZE AVAILABILITY CHART

Male Sizes	2	3	4	5	6	7	8	9	10	11
Female Sizes		4	5	6	7	8	9	10		
Super Pro	x	x	x	x	x	x	x		x	x
Sport Pro	x	x	x	x	x	x	x		x	x
Junior Pro	x	x	x	x	x	x	x			

Sizzler™

**All Sizzler™ skateboards
come equipped with:**
- The exclusive M.A.G. wheel and
truck system. (patents pending)
- 5/16" tempered steel axles
- Poured urethane tires
- Precision bearings

PHOTON™
Stock No. 1079
Standard Pack: 6
Weight/std. pk.: 20 lbs.
Deck: 22" x 6¼" polypropylene

FREESTYLER™
Stock No. 2547
Standard Pack: 6
Weight/std. pk.: 25 lbs.
Deck: 24" x 6½" laminated wood

ORANGE PEELER™
Stock No. 2525
Standard Pack: 6
Weight/std. pk.: 24 lbs.
Deck: 24" x 6½" polypropylene

YELLOW FLASH™
Stock No. 2526
Standard Pack: 6
Weight/std. pk.: 24 lbs.
Deck: 24" x 6½" polypropylene

SILVER SIZZLER™
Stock No. 1078
Standard Pack: 6
Weight/std. pk.: 25 lbs.
Deck: 24" x 6½" polypropylene

ROCK 'N ROLLER™
Stock No. 2546
Standard Pack: 6
Weight/std. pk.: 25 lbs.
Deck: 24" x 6½" laminated wood

INTELLiVISiON™
Intelligent Television

MATTEL ELECTRONICS®

Master Component Features

Mattel Electronics has engineered a single component that combines keypad, object and action controls.

Input keys with exclusive "overlay" system... Each game comes with customized printed overlays which fit directly over the keys. Game play without checking the instruction book.

Side mounted action buttons... Each controller has four action buttons—two on each side. For easy use by either right- or left-handed players.

Object control disk... Forget straight line joystick controllers for all time. On-screen objects can be precisely maneuvered in 16 different directions to simulate lifelike 360-degree movement.

Entertainment Networks

An ever-changing variety of play situations and player decisions are yours. No boredom here— whether you play against the computer or another player, there's always a challenge! Five cartridge networks can be used with the Master Component alone or with the Keyboard Component in combination.

Sports • Strategy • Children's Learning Fun • Action • Gaming

The Sports Network

MAJOR LEAGUE BASEBALL*

Field two 9-man teams for 9 full innings (extra innings if needed) of Major League Baseball excitement. It's all here, right down to the tumult of the crowd. Everything — walks, hit-and-runs, grand-slammers, a full variety of pitches — and you're in charge from the first pitch! Play ball!

*Trademark of and licensed by Major League Baseball Corp.

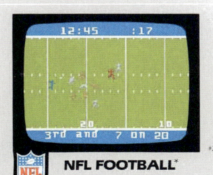

NFL FOOTBALL*

NFL action at your fingertips! Two animated teams. Two full halves. 60 exciting, simulated minutes of hard-hitting gridiron fun. Offense, defense, punts, passes, runs, computerized scoring, game sounds, music and much more. Every aspect of NFL competition has been electronically recreated to put you in the pressure cooker of big time football.

*Trademark of and licensed by National Football League Properties Inc.

The Intellivision home computer, from the Mattel Electronics Catalog, 1979.

ABOVE: Cover from the Mattel Catalog, 1979.
OPPOSITE: The Magical Musical Thing electronic synthesizer, from the Mattel Catalog, 1979.
FOLLOWING PAGES: Brain Baffler and Horoscope electronic games, from the Mattel Catalog, 1979.

#2967 MAGICAL MUSICAL THING Electronic Instrument

MATTEL MUSIC

MAGICAL MUSICAL THING™

Touch a tune or stroke a song! Let your fingers move along! Our new Magical Musical Thing™ electronic instrument gives you music at a touch. With a 25-note scale and a tough & durable plastic casing – with the keyboard number and color-coded to the songbook which is included – we make doing your own thing a song! Play it like a piano keyboard. Play it like a guitar and be a star. Or create your own style that makes 'em smile. Just run your hands along the neck, or rub it gently over your clothed body. Operates on 9-volt battery, not included.
#2967 Std. Pak 6/Wt. 9 lbs.

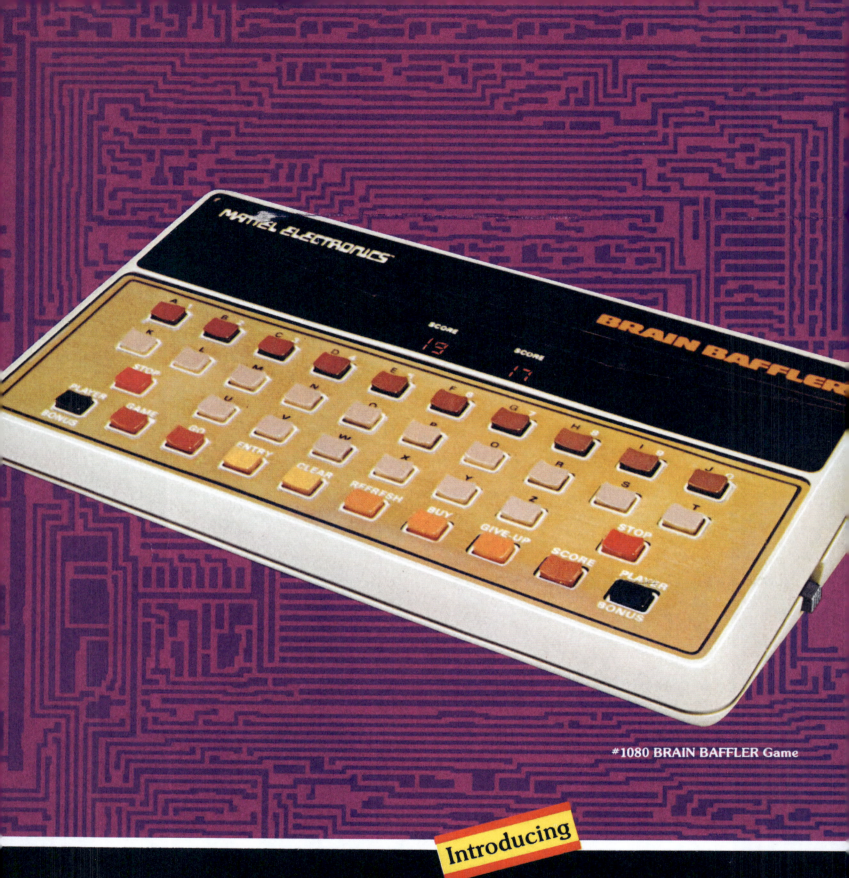

#1080 BRAIN BAFFLER Game

Introducing

MATTEL ELECTRONICS™

Mattel Electronics™ presents a diversified line of fine quality pocket electronic products. Through the use of the latest microelectronics technology, each self-contained product offers unlimited fun and challenge right in the palm of your hand. No TV set needed. The best in major sports, action and strategy game themes. Each product comes fully assembled with built-in simulated sound effects, precision lens, digital scoring, L.E.D. display, electronic printed circuits and complete playing instructions. Each operates on 9-volt transistor battery, not included

Brain Baffler™

The electronic wizard that plays games with human minds! Match wit with an opponent or against the built-in thinking computer! The computer controls the action, scoring, game play, plus new variations for the most challenging and popular strategy word and number games Go Hang™…Mixed-Up Words™…Build-A-Word™…Flash Words™ …Third Degree Anagrams™…and Copy That™ games! Educational as well as entertaining. Advanced micro-computer technology makes i possible for you to enjoy all of these games, anytime, anyplace! You'l have to sharpen your wits for this one!
#1080 Std. Pak 6/Wt. 4 lbs.

#1081 HOROSCOPE COMPUTER Game

NOW AVAILABLE:
Mattel Electronics™ AC Adapter designed for game use without the need for batteries. Compatible with all 9-volt battery operated Mattel Electronics™ games with AC adapter jack. Now enjoy computerized fun with or without batteries. Note: Do not attempt to re-charge batteries with Mattel Electronics™ AC Adapter. Adapter serves as a battery eliminator only.
#1103 Std. Pak 24/Wt. 10 lbs.

Introducing

Horoscope Computer™

Unlock the secrets of the stars with this quick, easy way to get a computer analysis of your horoscope. Enter your exact birthdate and the current date and get answers about Love...Money...Career...Family... Friends...Travel...Spirit...Creativity in your life! Computer answers based on authentic astrological calculations. Then you decide what to do. Even matches compatibility! Valid for three years—from May 31, 1979 to June 1, 1982!!
FOR ENTERTAINMENT PURPOSES ONLY!
#1081 Std. Pak 6/Wt. 4 lbs.

CRISS CROSS CRASH

#2945 CRISS-CROSS CRASH Set
Set not for use with all HOT WHEELS cars.

71

Avoid the crash!
Make it around the track!

Big trouble at the crossover! Only you at the Drive Wheel can prevent it! Two Hot Wheels® cars are streaking straight for the intersection. You crank the wheel, time it perfectly, avoid a crash! Cars make it around the track. Criss-Cross Crash™ set gives you two Hot Wheels cars, crossover and Drive Wheel power unit. No batteries needed. Three 15-inch track sections & one 9¾-inch section included. Plus curves & track supports, decals & instructions. Package has 4-color art. Assembly required.
#2945 Std. Pak 6/Wt. 20 lbs.

Hot Wheels Criss Cross Crash track set, from the Mattel Catalog, 1979.

The Heroes™

Six cartoon specials! Hot Wheels® vehicles with your favorite Marvel Comics characters–such as "Captain America"™, "Thor"™ & "The Thing"™ prominently displayed. "Spider-Man's" car, too! All The Heroes™ vehicles are die-cast metal. Blister cards have 4-colors.

#2877 Std. Pak 12/Wt. 2 lbs.
#2878 Std. Pak 12/Wt. 2 lbs.
#2879 Std. Pak 12/Wt. 2 lbs.
#2880 Std. Pak 12/Wt. 2 lbs.
#2881 Std. Pak 12/Wt. 2 lbs.
#2882 Std. Pak 12/Wt. 2 lbs.
#2883 Asst. Pak 72/Wt. 9 lbs.

©1978 Marvel Comics Group, division of Cadence Industries Corp. All Rights Reserved. 'Trademarks of Marvel Comics Group.

THE HEROES Vehicles

#2877 SPIDER-MAN*

#2880 THOR

#2881 HUMAN TORCH*

#2879 CAPTAIN AMERICA

#2878 THE INCREDIBLE HULK*

#2882 THE THING

HOT WHEELS SCENE MACHINES Vehicles

#2853 (Recreational)

#2855 (Space)

#2851 Captain America

#2850 The Incredible Hulk

#2852 Spider-Man

#2854 S.W.A.T. Van

Look inside! See a fun picture! Now there's a line of Hot Wheels® vans & cars with a neat scene inside. Hold 'em up and see "Spider-Man"™, "Captain America"™, or "The Incredible Hulk"™! Recreational, S.W.A.T. and Space scenes, too! 4-color blister cards are self-demonstrators. Hurry, hurry to the big Scene Machines™ picture show!
#2859 Asst. Only 72/Wt. 14 lbs. 8 oz.

68

Hot Wheels Scene Machines, from the Mattel Catalog, 1979.

Sport & Shave™ Ken®

It's Ken® with a whole new look for 1980! He's athletic. He's all man. He even "shaves"! Kids can draw a beard on his face, then "shave" it off. Again and again. Or draw funny mustaches. It's fun! They can pretend he's a tennis star or marathon runner with or without a mustache. He's got a big date with glamorous Barbie® doll and he's been working out all day. Never fear — everything's included to help him get ready. Our man Ken comes with beard marker, shaving mug, 2 "shavers", after shave/cologne bottle, toothbrush, toothpaste tube, hairbrush, comb, hair dryer, wristwatch, tennis racket, jacket, shorts, long pants, shoes. 4-color chip package.
#1294 Std. Pak 12

4

#1294 SPORT & SHAVE KEN doll

Draw on a beard.

Help him "shave" it off!

Tennis star

Date with Barbie®

Grooming gear galore!

©Mattel, Inc. 1980

Sport 'n' Shave Ken doll, from the Mattel Movin' Ahead Catalog, 1980.

SUN LOVIN' malibu. Dolls

The dolls with the peek-a-boo tans! Barbie®, Skipper®, Christie®, P.J.®, and Ken® have real tan lines as if they'd been in the sun. Each comes with "mirrored" sunglasses in the latest fashion shape, beach bag and monogrammed swimsuit. All dolls are poseable. Each sold separately.

#1067 Std. Pak 12 #7745 Std. Pak 12
#1069 Std. Pak 12 #1187 Std. Pak 12
#1088 Std. Pak 12

6

Black Barbie®

Black is beautiful, and Black Barbie® is a knock-out! She's ready for a night out in her fabulous bodysuit with wrap-&-snap disco skirt. Little girls will love to pose Barbie. Her arms move and she twists at the waist. Completing the outfit, she comes with stylish haircomb/pick, stud, hoop & dangle earrings, modern necklace & ring, and shoes. 4-color chip window package.
#1293 Std. Pak 6

#7745
SUN LOVIN'
MALIBU
CHRISTIE Doll

#1187
SUN LOVIN'
MALIBU P.J. Doll

#1088
SUN LOVIN'
MALIBU KEN Doll

#1067
SUN LOVIN'
MALIBU BARBIE Doll

#1069
SUN LOVIN'
MALIBU SKIPPER Doll

Suntan lines!
Beach bag!
Dazzling "mirrored" sunglasses!

#1293 Black BARBIE Doll

Fun accessories for Black Barbie Doll

©Mattel, Inc. 1980

#1292 Hispanic BARBIE Doll

©Mattel, Inc. 1980

ABOVE: The introduction of Black Barbie, from the Mattel Movin' Ahead Catalog, 1980.
FOLLOWING PAGES: The Masters of the Universe Castle Grayskull set, from the Mattel Catalog, 1982.

MASTERS OF THE UNIVERSE

New For 82!

From a fabulous age of heroes, these finely detailed action figures provide a new world of fantasy! Castle Grayskull™ is the center-piece of the collection, filled with secrets that bring the imagination to life. He-man™ is the strongest man in the universe. His allies are Man-at-Arms™ and Teela,™ a warrior goddess. Their enemies are Skeletor™ and Beast Man.™ Others join in the battles for the castle: Mer-man,™ Stratos™ and Zodac™ are warriors of the sea and sky. Action figures are 5 ½″ tall, and articulated to deliver a "power punch". Blister packed. Each sold separately.

Also shown are Wind Raider,™ Battle Ram™ and Battle Cat.™ **Ages 5 and over.**
#5050 Asst. Pak 24 (includes #5040-5043)
#5334 Asst. Pak 24 (includes #5044-5047)
#5335 Asst. Pak 36 (includes #5040-5047)
#5040 Std. Pak 12   #5044 Std. Pak 12
#5041 Std. Pak 12   #5045 Std. Pak 12
#5042 Std. Pak 12   #5046 Std. Pak 12
#5043 Std. Pak 12   #5047 Std. Pak 12

Castle Grayskull™
Castle Grayskull™ accessories and features include a "jawbridge" that opens and closes, working trapdoor and elevator, castle throne, weapons collection, combat trainer, cannon and flag. Folds in half for easy carrying. Size 18″ x 27″. Some assembly required. Corrugated with 4-color label. **Ages 5 and over.**
#3991 Std. Pak 4

#3991 CASTLE GRAYSKULL
Fortress of mystery and power

#5047 STRATOS
Winged warrior

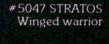

#5046 MER-MAN
Ocean warlord

#5040 HE-MAN
Strongest man in the universe

#5117 WIND RAIDER
Assault lander

#5044 ZODAC
Cosmic enforcer

#5048 BATTLE CAT
Fighting tiger

The Castle folds for easy carrying

#5042 SKELETOR
Lord of destruction

#5041 MAN-AT-ARMS
Master of weapons

#5045 TEELA
Warrior goddess

#5043 BEAST MAN
Savage henchman

#3990 BATTLE RAM
Mobile launcher

© Mattel. Inc. 1982

MATTEL

71

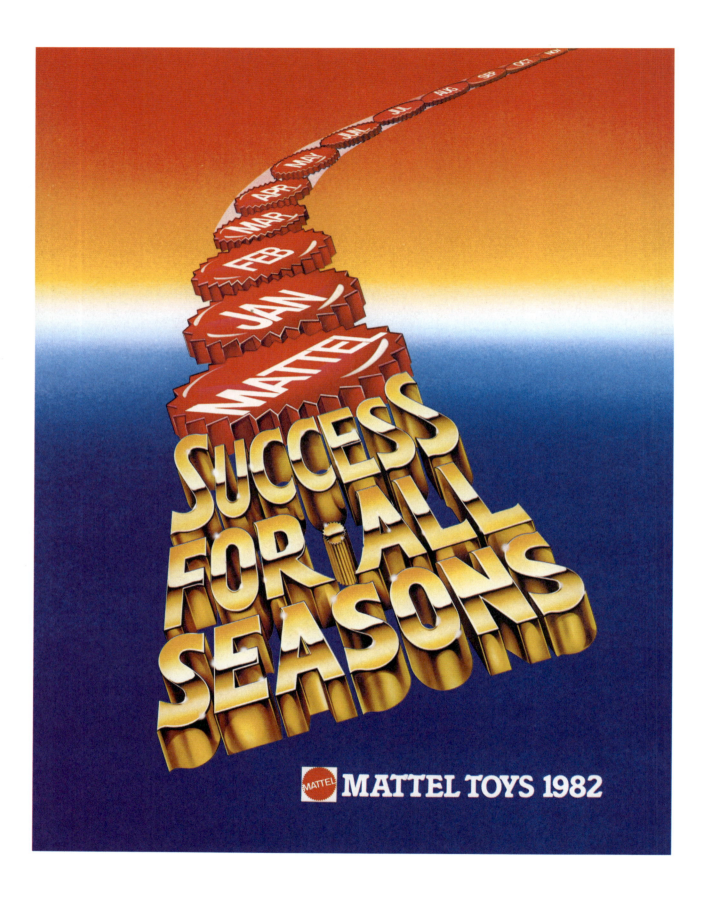

ABOVE: Cover from the Mattel Catalog, 1982.
OPPOSITE: Cover and Hot Wheels pages from the Mattel Catalog, 1983.

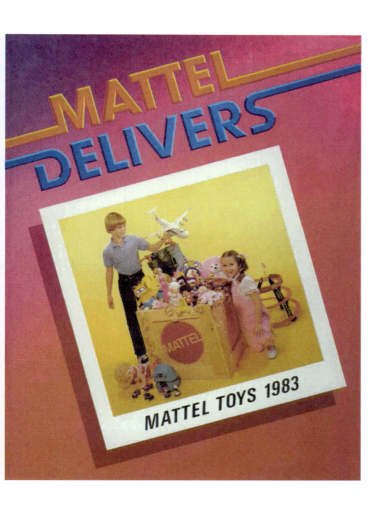

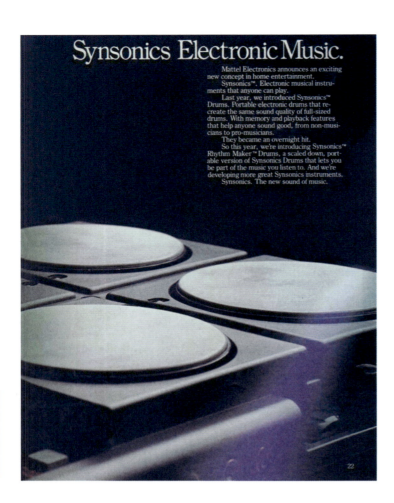

Synsonics Electronic Music.

Mattel Electronics announces an exciting new concept in home entertainment. Synsonics™. Electronic musical instruments that anyone can play.

Last year, we introduced Synsonics™ Drums. Portable electronic drums that recreate the same sound quality of full-sized drums. With memory and playback features that help anyone sound good, from non-musicians to pro-musicians.

They became an overnight hit.

So this year, we're introducing Synsonics™ Rhythm Maker™ Drums, a scaled down, portable version of Synsonics Drums that lets you be part of the music you listen to. And we're developing more great Synsonics instruments.

Synsonics. The new sound of music.

22

Intellivision® Entertainment Computer System, Page 65

LOCK 'N' CHASE

video computer system™

M Network™ Compatible Software, Page 33

Aquarius™ Home Computer System.
Smart enough to be simple.

Introducing the home computer system that's so sophisticated, it makes home computing simple.

The Aquarius Home Computer System. The simplicity starts at the Aquarius Home Computer, with straight forward plug-in operation and Simplified Instruction Cards. Plus the built-in Microsoft™* BASIC language for more flexible program commands. You can actually start writing your first computer program in minutes. The Aquarius System is also easy to expand because of its unique plug-in memory cartridges and its full line of peripherals. (Each sold separately.)

The Aquarius Home Computer is even easy to afford.

But don't let the simplicity of Aquarius fool you. It's a sophisticated home computer system with advanced capabilities and features. Including the powerful Z80A microprocessor. A 16-color display with outstanding graphic resolution. Memory capability of up to 52K RAM (Random Access Memory). Even the versality to expand into one of the largest applications software libraries, through its CP/M®** operating capability.

And Aquarius has a big software library to help you do simply amazing things.

Manage home finances or organize important family information like important dates. Help your children learn computer programming and basic subjects in a fun and simple way. Or, learn advanced programming skills. Aquarius even has a big selection of video games.

The Aquarius Home Computer System. It's versatile, flexible and powerful. Best of all, it's simple.

*Master Component, voice module and cartridges each sold separately.

Aquarius™ specifications and features.	
Memory:	Z80A
Program Language:	Microsoft™ BASIC
Memory:	8K ROM, 4K RAM, (User Expandable to 52K)
Colors:	16
Display:	320 x 192 Graphic Resolution, 40 x 24 Character Display, 256 Total Characters including the complete ASCII set with upper and lower case letters, numbers, plus additional graphic symbols.
Keyboard:	49 Moving Keys
Dimensions:	13" x 6" x 2"
Weight:	68 oz.

*"Microsoft"™ is a trademark of Microsoft Corporation.
**"CP/M" is a registered trademark of Digital Research, Inc.

3

4

Cover and pages from the Mattel Electronics Catalog, 1983.

In touch with Tomorrow.

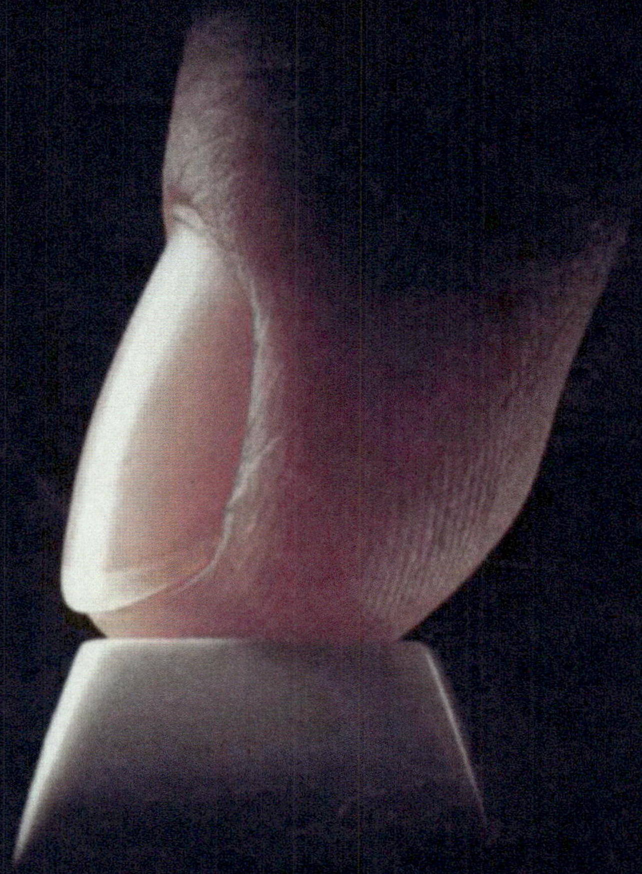

MATTEL ELECTRONICS®

1983 Catalog

Get more mileage in 1983 from Fisher-Price Ride Ons

Ride-Ons, from the Fisher-Price Catalog, 1983.

PRESCHOOL

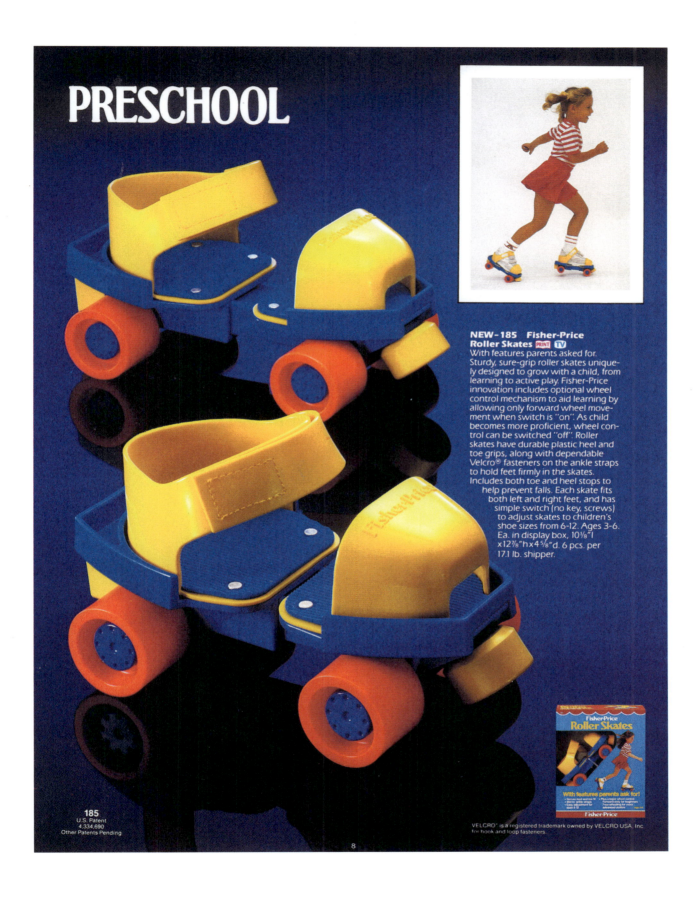

**NEW–185 Fisher-Price
Roller Skates** PRINT TV
With features parents asked for.
Sturdy, sure-grip roller skates unique-
ly designed to grow with a child, from
learning to active play. Fisher-Price
innovation includes optional wheel
control mechanism to aid learning by
allowing only forward wheel movement when switch is "on". As child
becomes more proficient, wheel control can be switched "off". Roller
skates have durable plastic heel and
toe grips, along with dependable
Velcro® fasteners on the ankle straps
to hold feet firmly in the skates.
Includes both toe and heel stops to
help prevent falls. Each skate fits
both left and right feet, and has
simple switch (no key, screws)
to adjust skates to children's
shoe sizes from 6-12. Ages 3-6.
Ea. in display box, 10⅛"l
x12⅞"h x4⅝"d. 6 pcs. per
17.1 lb. shipper.

185
U.S. Patent
4,334,690
Other Patents Pending

8

VELCRO® is a registered trademark owned by VELCRO USA, Inc.
for hook and loop fasteners.

Roller-Skates, from the Fisher-Price Catalog, 1984.

Pages from the Mattel Emotions Catalog, 1984.

"Boy, I must be the luckiest kid in the world."

THE WESTLEY DOG FAMILY
Cleverly stitched and tucked, these droopy-lidded pets have a talent for cheering people up.

G 1000 WESTLEY BABY Size 5½" H
G 1001 WESTLEY   Size 6½" H
G 1002 WESTLEY SR.   Size 9½" H

"look daddy, i'm a Boo Hoo Hoo too!"

THE BOO HOO HOO FAMILY
There's never been anything like it! Each of these lovable, cuddly softies wears *a permanent crystal-like teardrop*—an EMOTIONS exclusive so unusual, it attracts everyone's eye

G 1073 BOO HOO HOO BEAR Size 9" H
G 1074 BOO HOO HOO DOG Size 8" H

Mattel Toys 1985

Day-to-Night Barbie

Dressed for day

Dressed for night

Barbie® is ready for the bright city life. Her beautiful suit becomes a glamorous gown! By day, Barbie has an exciting career. She's everything today's little girl dreams of being. And her pretty pink suit and hat are perfect for the job. She even has an attaché case filled with things like a play calculator, "magazines" and her very own business card. After five, girls can remove her jacket, reverse her skirt, change her shoes, and she's ready for a night on the town. Day-to-Night™ Barbie® doll's glamorous life just goes on and on! Our 11½" doll comes with suit jacket, bodysuit, reversible skirt, hat, scarf, 2 pairs of shoes, attaché case, shoulder bag, jewelry, play calculator, brush, comb, labels, and these package punchouts: Barbie business card, child-size business card, 2 play magazines, newspaper, Barbie credit card. 4-color chip window package.

For ages over 3.   7929 Std. Pak 12
Not Shown:
Black DAY-TO-NIGHT BARBIE Doll
7945 Std. Pak 12
Hispanic DAY-TO-NIGHT
BARBIE Doll
7944 Std. Pak 12

**Day-to-Night™
KEN®**
Change his look from day to night, too. Ken® comes with shirt/pants with vest, jacket and business tie, shirt front/bow tie/cummerbund, shoes, socks and package punchouts: credit card, business card, 2 play magazines, newspaper, child-size business card. 4-color chip window package.

For ages over 3.   9019 Std. Pak 12
Not Shown:
Black DAY-TO-NIGHT™ KEN®Doll
9018 Std. Pak 12

ADVERTISED ON TV

At the office

9019 DAY-TO-NIGHT KEN Doll

7929 DAY-TO-NIGHT BARBIE Doll

Accessories galore!

Day to Night Barbie, which debuted in the Mattel Catalog, 1985.

SLIME PIT™
New! TV advertising! Even more frightening than the Fright Zone®, more terrifying than Snake Mountain! This evil pit of gruesome ooze has a fearsome claw that can trap a warrior. The skull-head opens up to coat the warrior with Slime®. Slime compound, comic book and "care and feeding" brochure included. Figure not included. Four-color box.
9989 SLIME PIT   STD. PAK 12

SLIME®
New! TV advertising! It's cold, clammy and gooey. 6 fl. oz., non-toxic water soluble gel in a resealable can.
2487 SLIME   STD. PAK 48

Slime Pit and Slime are not for use with flocked or battery powered Masters of the Universe® toys.

MONSTROID™
New! TV advertising! This fearsome mechanical creature can whirl and spin, knocking down approaching warriors. And, its awesome pincers can hold prisoners tightly. When wound up, it can spin up to 20 seconds. No batteries are needed. Not for use with some Masters of the Universe figures. Figures not included. Four-color box.
2418 MONSTROID   STD. PAK 6

2487 SLIME Gel

2418 MONSTROID Creature

9989 SLIME PIT Play Set

175

ABOVE: The Masters of the Universe Slime Pit set, from the Mattel Catalog, 1986.
FOLLOWING PAGES: The introduction of She-Ra, Princess of Power, in the Mattel Catalog, 1985.

Princess of POWER™

DOLL COLLECTION

Glamour! Fashion! Adventure! All tied into one exciting line of fashion dolls — She-Ra™ and the Princess of Power™ collection. Here are the dolls little girls will be telling you about! Beautiful 5½" fashion dolls, each with a glamorous fashion look and a unique, magical action feature. More than just a beautiful face, each doll has long, combable hair, and spectacular costumes that are removable for exciting fantasy fashion play. All dolls come with a comic book story for hours of imaginative play. Each sold separately. 4-color chip blister cards.

For ages 4 and over.
9182 - 9190 Std. Pak 12
9238 Asst. Pak 24

ADVERTISED ON TV

Each sold separately.

NEW '85

Action waist _ _
"I have the power!"

9187 CASTASPELLA™
Enchantress who hypnotizes!

She casts a "magical spell" with her spinning disc!

9182 SHE-RA™
Beautiful Princess Adora™ becomes She-Ra, most powerful woman in the Universe!

9188 GLIMMER®
The guide who lights the way!

9186 ANGELLA™
Angellic winged guide!

Her angel wings take her to the heavens!

Her headdress and staff glow in the dark!

46

© Mattel, Inc. 198

9183 BOW™
Special friend who helps She-Ra!

Turn the wheel behind her back ... see her other face!

9185 DOUBLE TROUBLE™
Glamorous double agent!

sh button on his back ... his heart ats" for She-Ra!

9184 CATRA™
Jealous beauty!

Ask him a question. Lift his secret panel for one of three color-coded answers!

9189 FROSTA™
Ice Empress of Etheria™

9190 KOWL™
The know-it-owl!

With her glamorous mask and action waist, she becomes a purrrfect "cat!"

Her snowflake wand spins and whistles like the wind!

© Mattel, Inc. 1985

MATTEL

47

"You are the hero *of your own story.*"

American Girl, 1986

CHAPTER FOUR

Pushing Play Forward

In the 1980s, it seemed like bigger was always better. Mattel embraced that philosophy, putting out some of its largest and all-encompassing toy catalogs as the 1980s drew to a close.

Mattel continued to invest heavily in Barbie, expanding offerings across all price points to ensure there was a Barbie that suited every child. They even put out the very first collector's edition Barbie with Holiday Barbie in 1988, a deluxe holiday-themed line that has topped holiday wish lists since the line's debut through to the present day.

1986–1998

THE AMERICAN GIRLS COLLECTION
Spring 1990

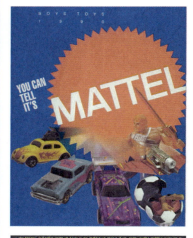

YOU CAN TELL IT'S MATTEL

TOYFAIR 1997

Fisher-Price
Showroom Guide

GIRLS TOYS 1992

MATTEL

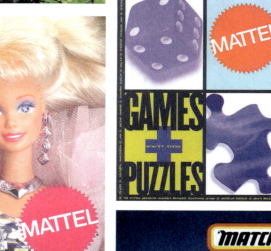

MATTEL

GAMES + PUZZLES

setting the pace

MATTEL

Mattel Toys 1988

Pleasant Company
Bookseller Catalogue

JOSEFINA MONTOYA
New Mexico 1824

New!
Josefina Books & Sidelines

Family Album & Party Book

Five New Titles

We've made American girls our business!

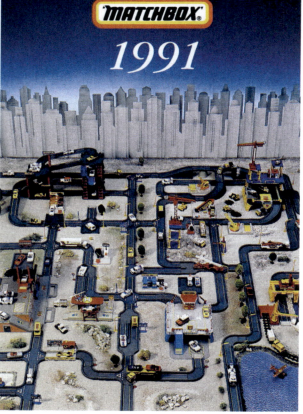

MATCHBOX
1991

Barbie and the Rockers, a series of Barbie dolls, fashions, and a stage playset, inspired Mattel's first Barbie animated special of the same name. Barbie's dominance of the toy industry could not be ignored, and, in 1989, Ruth and Elliot Handler became the first living creators to receive the honor of being inducted into the Toy Industry Hall of Fame, for Barbie and all of the other amazing toys they had created at Mattel. In 1992, Totally Hair Barbie premiered and became Mattel's most successful Barbie to date.

But Mattel was never a company to rest on past successes. Determined to keep growing and pushing play forward with new toys, Mattel realized that they needed to acquire other toymakers. They purchased ARCO Industries, a production company in Hong Kong, to produce Barbie playsets; the French dollmakers Corolle S.A.; Corgi Toys; sports toy company Aviva; baby and pre-school toy maker Fisher-Price; international rights to the game Scrabble from J.W. Spear & Sons; and Kransco, who produced Power Wheels, Hula Hoops, and Frisbee, adding all of these iconic brands and toys to Mattel catalogs. Mattel purchased the rights to produce Cabbage Patch Dolls and then absorbed Tyco Toys in 1997, bringing in brands such as Matchbox, View-Master, and Magic 8 Ball. Following Tyco, Mattel acquired International Games, a small company that produced popular card games like UNO and Skip Bo. Two years later, Mattel purchased Bluebird Toys PLC of the UK, the creators of Polly Pocket.

Thanks to all of these acquisitions and mergers, Mattel was bigger than ever before, producing a much wider range of toys that served almost every demographic of childhood. The only thing missing from their impressive catalogs was a doll line for girls who were growing out of Barbie, but weren't quite ready to give up on imaginative play.

The solution? American Girl.

In 1998, Mattel acquired Pleasant Company, a company that made and sold historical-based dolls via catalog. These 18-inch dolls sold alongside clothing, accessory and furniture sets, and award-winning books about each doll that helped girls see how strong they could be and how much they could accomplish. Already popular with elementary-aged girls, Mattel's acquisition of the brand allowed American Girl to scale quickly, adding additional doll options, opening brick-and-mortar stores, and expanding American Girl into a wholesome, inspirational lifestyle brand that girls embraced.

OPPOSITE, CLOCKWISE FROM UPPER LEFT: Covers from The American Girl Collection, 1986; Mattel Boys' Toys Catalog, 1990; Fisher-Price Showroom Guide, 1997; Mattel Games and Puzzles Catalog, 1997; Mattel Catalog, 1986; Matchbox Collector's Catalog, 1991; Pleasant Company Bookseller Catalog, 1998; and Mattel Girls' Toys Catalog, 1992.

Catalog Archive

Simulated TV picture

ABOVE: The Masters of the Universe card game, from the Mattel Catalog, 1986.
FOLLOWING PAGES: The Masters of the Universe Eternia set, from the Mattel Catalog, 1986.

ETERNIA™

New! This is the ultimate battle ground — the biggest, boldest Masters of the Universe set ever! It's an interactive toy with many working parts for children to operate and lots of surprise elements. One of the most exciting features is the tram that runs throughout Eternia. Three different vehicles can run on the tram-way: a jet pack, a cage and a gondola. When attached to the power module, each of them becomes a motorized tram car. In addition to the tram, each of the towers is filled with exciting features. Grayskull Tower has a dungeon with a working door that works automatically with the tram. Central Tower features a drawbridge that opens and closes plus a crank-turned elevator. And surrounding the tower is a moat that really holds water. The top floor of the Central Tower can be used as a landing support for the Fright Fighter™ vehicle (not included). This floor also features a cannon that can be mounted on the Blasterhawk™ vehicle (not included). The third tower is the Viper Tower which has a secret hideout and a vicious serpent head that children can remotely spin 360 degrees. For fun on an even larger scale, this sprawling fortress can be connected to Castle Grayskull and Snake Mountain, creating the entire world of Eternia™! Eternia™ also comes with flags, a weapons rack and an arsenal of weapons. Figures not included. Adult assembly required. Four-color box

2855 ETERNIA   STD. PAK 2

189

2855 ETERNIA Playset

Castle Grayskull and Snake Mountain sold separately

Cover and pages from the Mattel Emotions Catalog, Spring 1986.

The Holiday Celebration Barbie Special Edition doll, from the Mattel Barbie Collector Catalog, 2002. The original Holiday Barbie made her debut in 1988.

EARRING MAGIC™
TV BARBIE® DOLLS

Barbie and her friends provide cool earring fashion fun for you! Included with both Barbie and Midge® are charms to attach to earrings or waist belt. Plus, child-size earrings are included so little girls can wear charms, too! Girl dolls' dresses are in hot colors with netting bodice and sleeves. Even Ken® wears an earring and has a Barbie and a Ken charm, too! Ken doll also includes child-size earrings. For ages 3 years and over.
12¾"H x 5"W x 2⅜"D WINDOW BOX
7014 STD. PAK 12 (BARBIE DOLL)
10255 STD. PAK 6 (BRUNETTE DOLL)
2374 STD. PAK 6 (BLACK DOLL)
10256 STD. PAK (MIDGE DOLL)
2290 STD. PAK 6 (KEN DOLL)

EARRING MAGIC™
BARBIE® FASHIONS
ASSORTMENT

Four cool fashions in bright colors with charms that provide fashion jewelry fun for Barbie and earring fun for you! Each fashion comes with vacuum-metalized child-size earrings and charms. The charms can be worn as earrings for the girl or as charms for Barbie doll's costume. Dolls not included. For ages 3 years and over.
12"H x 9"W BLISTER CARD
A4628 ASST. PAK 24

Includes charms and earrings both Barbie and girls can wear!

Includes one pair child-size earrings!

10255 EARRING MAGIC Brunette BARBIE Doll

A4528 EARRING MAGIC BARBIE Fashions Assortment

2374 EARRING MAGIC Black BARBIE Doll

10256 EARRING MAGIC Midge Doll

2290 EARRING MAGIC Ken Doll

7014 EARRING MAGIC BARBIE Doll

4523 4525 4527 4526

Earring Magic Barbie, from the Mattel Girls' Toys Catalog, 1993.

GLITTER BEACH™
BARBIE® DOLL
TV & FRIENDS

Barbie and her friends are the hottest dolls on the beach in their trendy floral swimsuits that glitter with a hot flashy look! Plus, there's more glitter fun with the magic glitter lotion that makes Barbie and girls glitter from head-to-toe. Barbie doll and her friends all have beautiful long hair, "gemstone" necklaces, sparkling earrings and matching glitter bandanas. Ken® and Steven® wear glittery floral swim trunks, muscle shirts and surfer charm necklaces. For ages 3 years and over.
12¾"H x 3½"W x 1⅜"D WINDOW BOX
11½"H x 3½"W x 1⅜"D WINDOW BOX
(SKIPPER® DOLL ONLY)
4920 STD. PAK 6 (A. SKIPPER DOLL)
4507 STD. PAK 6 (B. CHRISTIE® DOLL)
4935 STD. PAK 6 (C. JAZZIE® DOLL)
4921 STD. PAK 6 (D. TERESA® DOLL)
4804 STD. PAK 6 (E. KEN DOLL)
3602 STD. PAK 12 (F. BARBIE DOLL)
4918 STD. PAK 6 (G. STEVEN DOLL)
4924 STD. PAK 6 (H. KIRA® DOLL)

Glitter Beach lotion for Barbie and you!

Glitter Beach Barbie, from the Mattel Girls' Toys Catalog, 1993.

New Fisher-Price Fun with Food. Everything it takes to get a kid's imagination cookin'.

CONTENTS

COLOR RACERS™ 3-Car Paks

Check out these Hot Wheels cars! Now you can "paint" your cars like magic! Just dip your Color Racers cars into icy cold or warm tap water and watch them change color instantly right before your eyes! You can paint them again and again! Details like racing stripes and numbers change! Create two-tone paint jobs! Some vehicles not for use with some sets. Vehicles may vary from those shown. 4-color blister card. For ages over 5.

5615 ASST. PAK 24

COLOR RACERS 3-CAR PAKS

5600

5607

1440

1439

5605

5608

188

1986–1998

PREVIOUS PAGES: Fun with Food, from the Fisher-Price Catalog, 1987.
ABOVE AND FOLLOWING PAGES: Hot Wheels Color Racers and the Color Racers Auto Paint Factory, from the Mattel Catalogs, 1989 and 1988 respectively.
OPPOSITE: The introduction of Captain Power, from the Mattel Catalog, 1987.

5790 COLOR RACERS Auto Paint

![Hot Wheels logo]

20TH ANNIVERSARY
ANNIVERSARY
1968 — 1988
SPECIAL COLLECTOR'S EDITION

Happy Anniversary Hot Wheels! For the millions of kids
have grown up with the Hot Wheels family of cars and tru
1988 marks the 20th year of product innovation and quali.
...And the excitement continues! In addition to the Specia
Collector's Edition (not shown), 1988 marks the introduct
of the all new COLOR RACERS™ color change cars! Nov
Wheels cars change color instantly, again and again! All
Wheels vehicles and sets are for ages over 3 except where n

103

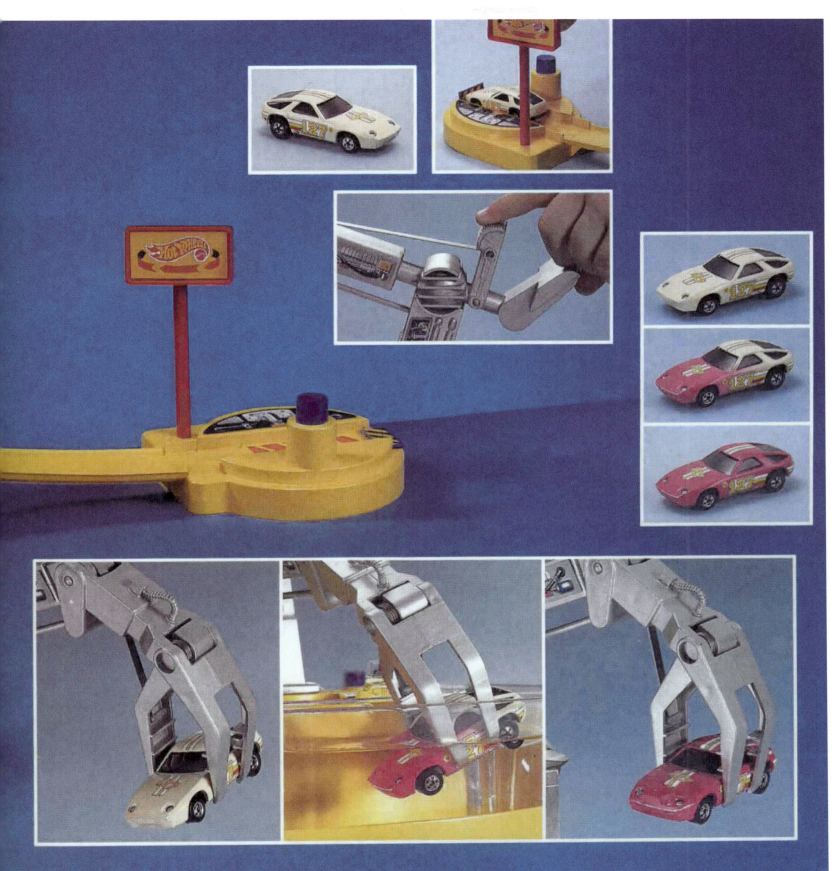

© Mattel, Inc. 1988

COLOR RACERS™ AUTO PAINT FACTORY

New! TV ADVERTISING! Everything you need to create custom paint jobs is included! Cars *really* change color! All it takes is water! No paint mess! Use crane to submerge car in "paint tanks" of icy cold or warm water for solid color paint jobs! Or "dip" just the hood for a two-toned effect! Cars change color instantly, just like magic! Auto Paint Factory includes drip tray, elevator, turntable, water bins, ramp, "spin dryer", launcher, one Color Racers car, and label sheet. Everything stores inside! For use only with Color Racers cars.
4-color closed box. For ages over 5.

5790 • STD. PAK 6

Pleasant company.

THE AMERICAN GIRLS COLLECTION

The first American Girl Collection catalog, 1986.

Pleasant T. Rowland, a native Midwesterner and children's textbook author, visited Colonial Williamsburg in the early 1980s. Impressed by how the town's living history museum brought history to life, Rowland wondered if there was a way to do the same thing using toys for girls; she ultimately founded Pleasant Company in 1986 with The American Girls Collection, which combined her love of American history and her commitment to high-quality educational products. Beginning with Kirsten Larson, Samantha Parkington, and Molly McIntire, each doll came with a book introducing her life and time period to readers. Buyers could then order additional historically accurate outfits, accessory packs, and furniture sets. The dolls were a resounding success, with sales growing from $1.7 million to $7.6 million worth of product within the first two years from launch, and setting the stage for many more American Girl dolls that continued to reflect different backgrounds, socio-economic groups, and historical time periods.

Mattel purchased Pleasant Company in 1998 and expanded the brand further, creating an even more diverse range of dolls and books that, through imaginative play and adventurous stories featuring courageous heroines, gives girls the chance to discover who they are—and who they're meant to be.

H E - M A N

He-Man® is the most powerful man in the universe! He-Man returns for 1990 with a muscular, contemporary look and the most realistic action feature Mattel has ever designed for a male action figure! New He-Man friends, enemies, vehicles, and accessories also join the lineup making the 1990 He-Man selection of toys the most fun and visually exciting ever! Watch for new episodes of the He-Man animated TV series and while you're at it . . . watch out for Skeletor!

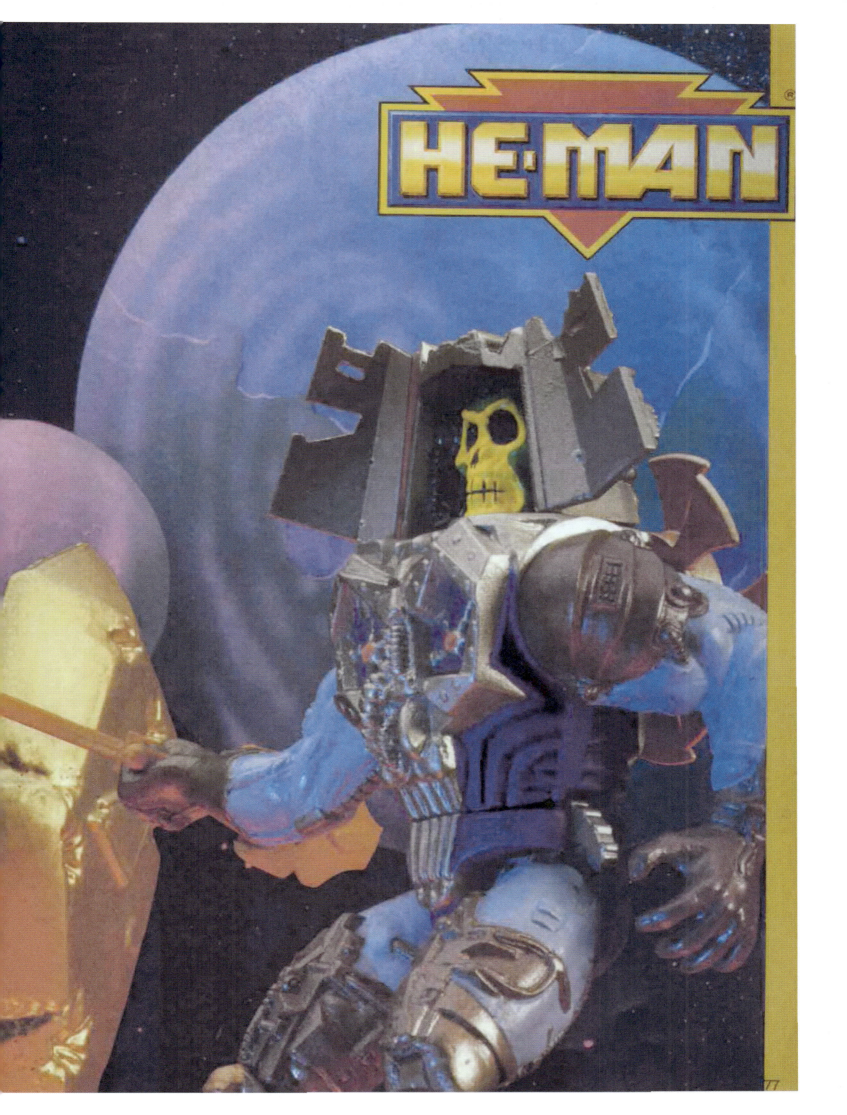

WITH OUR BILLIONTH CAR

INSTANT WINNING SWEEPSTAKES

1963 Classic Convertible Corvette OR $35,000 IN CASH

No purchase necessary. Details on package. Game ends 8/31/91.

4

Removable, raceable Corvette cars!

HOT WHEELS® BILLIONTH CAR COLLECTION™ NEW! A special collector edition! 4 die cast models of some of the hottest and fastest Corvette cars ever made. Each car comes complete with commemorative trophy to celebrate the production of over one billion quality Hot Wheels die cast cars. Great for display, or remove cars for some fast wheelin' racing action! Press-on letters make trophy easy to customize, and a special sweepstakes offer makes it possible to win a real '63 classic Corvette, $35,000, or thousands of other fabulous prizes. Sweepstakes ends August 31, 1991. Some cars not for use with some Hot Wheels sets. For ages 3 years and over. 12½"H x 5⅜"W x 2"D Window box.
9255 ASST. PAK 12

Corvette™ and Stingray trademarks licensed by Chevrolet Motor Division, General Motors Corporation.

9248 CUSTOM CORVETTE CONVERTIBLE
Styled for speed right down to the wheels!

9252 CORVETTE STINGRAY
A reproduction of one of the original 16 Hot Wheels cars released in 1968!

9254 SPLIT-WINDOW CORVETTE
A model of a rare collector's car with a distinctive rear window!

9258 CORVETTE HARDTOP
One of the most popular street models made!

5

1986-1998

HOT WHEELS

CALIFORNIA CUSTOMS

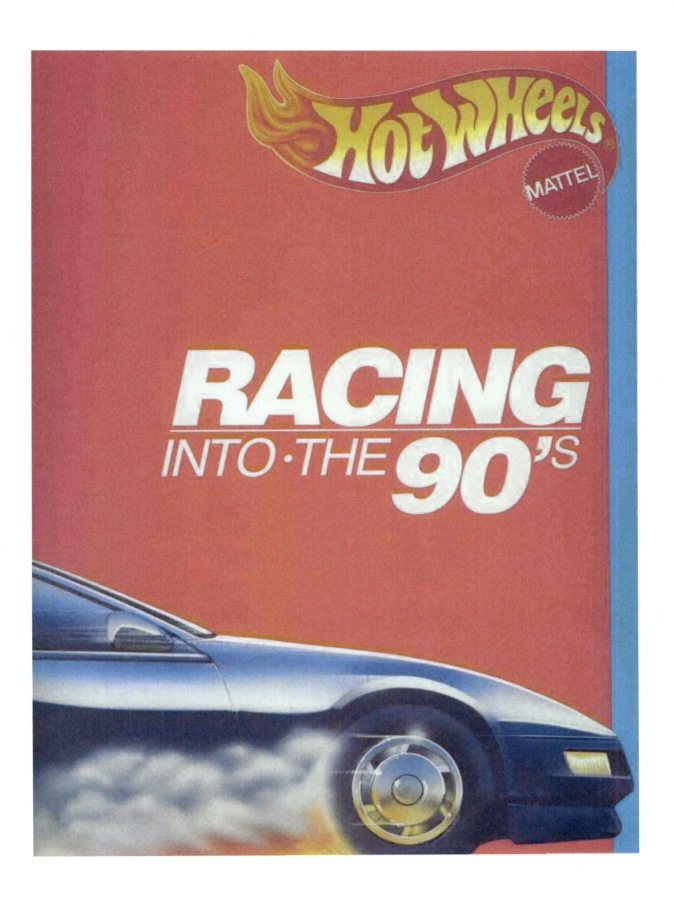

PREVIOUS PAGES: He-Man and Skeletor, from the Mattel Boys' Toys Catalog, 1990.
ABOVE AND OPPOSITE: Hot Wheels in the 1990s: the Billionth Car and the California Customs range, from the Mattel Boys' Toys Catalogs, 1990 and 1991.
FOLLOWING PAGES: ViewMaster 3-D Viewers, from the Tyco Catalog, 1990.

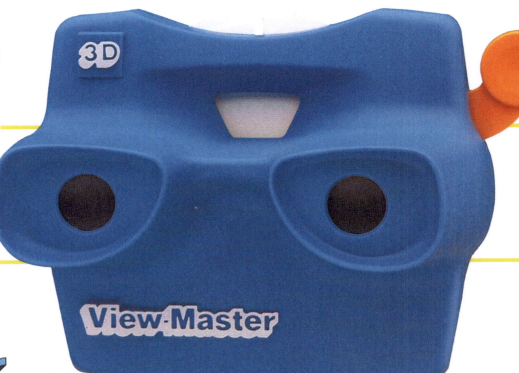

Standard 3-D Viewer
- A well-loved toy for more than 50 years!
- Advanced 3-D optical system.
- Sturdy, polystyrene viewer case.
- 2 eye-catching colors—bright red and electric blue.
- No batteries needed—easy to use.
- Carded package for easy display.
- Preview reel included.

Pkd 12 to master carton
4 lbs 5 oz; .60 cu ft

View-Master 3-D
VIEWERS

Push-Button Magenta Viewer
Stock No. 2060 ▼

Push-Button 3-D Viewer
- Award-winning contemporary design.
- Easy-to-use push-button advance.
- Supersize picture.
- Striking magenta and brilliant blue colors.
- Accommodates any View-Master reel.
- Kids can watch the reel revolve through transparent viewer back.
- Carded package.
- No batteries needed.
- Preview reel included.

Pkd 12 to master carton
4 lbs 8 oz; .85 cu ft

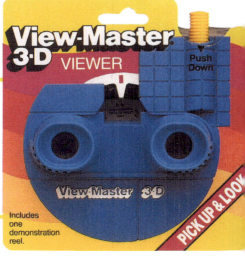

Includes one demonstration reel.

Standard Blue Viewer
Stock No. 2049

Standard Red Viewer
Stock No. 2050

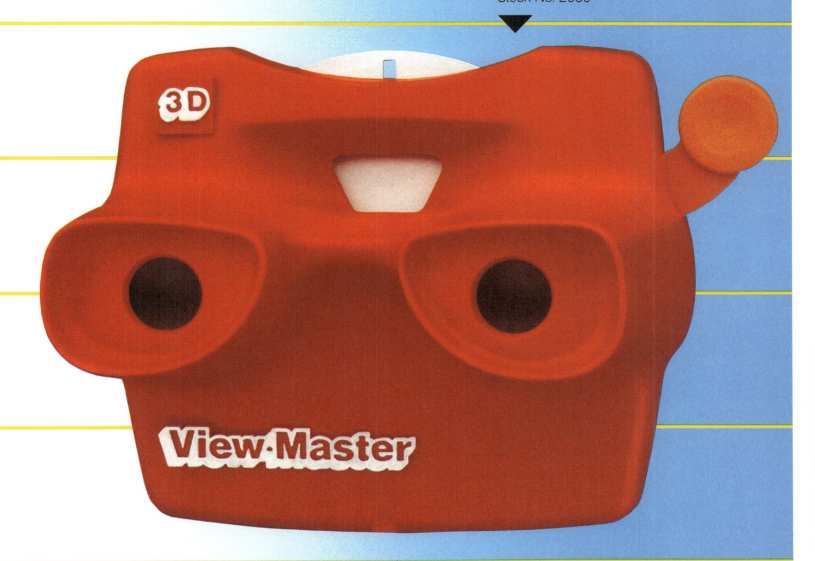

3D

View-Master

Standard Viewer Assortment
6 each red and blue viewers
Stock No. 2048

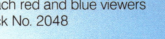

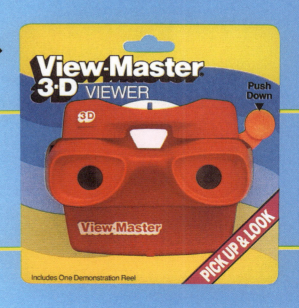

Push-Button Blue Viewer
Stock No. 2059

POWER GLOVE™ TURBO SPORT EDITION

NEW! It's lighter and quicker. With future-tech features that make it more than a match for any Nintendo Entertainment System game. The detachable, programmable keypad also doubles as a full-function controller with turbo and slow-motion controls built-in. The redesigned keypad delivers easier menu access, so players can jump into action sooner. It's more maneuverable and allows for even quicker reaction times for ultra-fast-paced games. For ages 8 years and over. Closed box.
4560 STD. PAK 4

SUPER GLOVE BALL™ GAME PAK

NEW! The revolutionary new game for the Nintendo Entertainment System that provides real "hands-on" action with spectacular 3-dimensional graphics. Players power their way through a maze of racquetball-like rooms by swatting a ball, as they avoid aliens, trapdoors, and an ever increasing number of threats. Super Glove Ball plays on a regular controller, or players can experience the game's amazing dimensional effects as they were designed for the Power Glove. Players curve the ball with "English" or fire robo-bullets with the bend of a finger. Only the Power Glove gives players an "intuitive control" of the game.
4522 STD. PAK 24

Power Glove is a trademark used under license.

Nintendo Entertainment System is a registered trademark of Nintendo of America Inc.

4560 POWER GLOVE Turbo Sport Edition

4522 SUPER GLOVE BALL Game Pak

200

1986-1998

The Power Glove video game accessory, from the Mattel Boys' Toys Catalog, 1990.

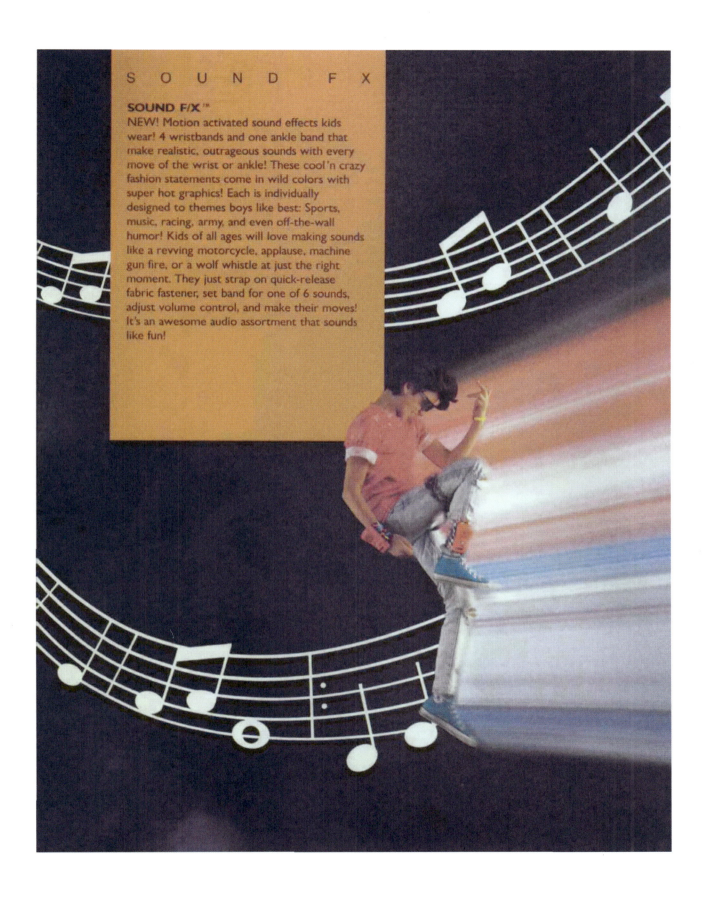

SOUND F X

SOUND F/X™

NEW! Motion activated sound effects kids wear! 4 wristbands and one ankle band that make realistic, outrageous sounds with every move of the wrist or ankle! These cool 'n crazy fashion statements come in wild colors with super hot graphics! Each is individually designed to themes boys like best: Sports, music, racing, army, and even off-the-wall humor! Kids of all ages will love making sounds like a revving motorcycle, applause, machine gun fire, or a wolf whistle at just the right moment. They just strap on quick-release fabric fastener, set band for one of 6 sounds, adjust volume control, and make their moves! It's an awesome audio assortment that sounds like fun!

Sound F/X wearable sound makers, from the Mattel Boys' Toys Catalog, 1990.

Barbie and Ken on the cover of the Arco Catalog, 1990.
OPPOSITE: The introduction of Totally Hair Barbie, in the Mattel Girls' Toys Catalog, 1992.

Totally Hair Barbie

NEW **TV**

TOTALLY HAIR™ BLONDE BARBIE® DOLL

Exciting news for '92! Totally Hair Barbie doll has the longest Barbie hair ever, 10½ inches! She's the ultimate in hairstyling fun! Comes with 5 new hair accessories, a chic Pucci-style outfit, shoes, hair pick, hairstyling booklet, Dep® Styling Gel, and a 55¢ coupon (while supplies last) off the next Dep Styling Gel purchase. (Coupon expires 3/31/93. See package for details.) For ages 3 years and over.

12¾"H x 6"W x 2⅜"D WINDOW BOX

A0769 ASST. PAK 12 (INCLUDES BLONDE & BRUNETTE DOLLS)
1112 STD. PAK 12 (BLONDE DOLLS ONLY)
5948 STD. PAK 6 (BLACK DOLL)

DEP is a trademark of and used with permission of Dep Corporation.

1112 TOTALLY HAIR
Blonde BARBIE Doll

11

Barbie®

New

EVENING EXTRAVAGANZA™ BARBIE® DOLL

Limited edition, from the Classique™ Collection for collectors, an exceptionally glamorous Barbie wearing an exquisitely detailed evening gown designed by Kitty Black Perkins. White Barbie wears a long, form-fitting strapless pink gown with sequins and a real, working zipper. Her wrap is iridescent pink and drapes gracefully over her shoulders to the floor. Her hair is curly, upswept and blonde and her lashes are rooted. Her accessories include a shimmering necklace with matching earrings and pink "satin" gloves. The black doll wears a gold dress with a gold wrap and gold gloves. Both dolls come with a doll stand and registration card in a package designed as a display piece. Age: fourteen years and older.

**14"H X 10"W X 3⅜"D
HINGED WINDOW BOX
11622 STD. PAK 4
WHITE BARBIE
11638 STD. PAK 4
BLACK BARBIE**

11638

11622

74

Evening Extravaganza Barbie, from the Mattel Girls' Toys Catalog, 1994.

SOUL TRAIN SHANI® DOLL & FRIENDS

There's lots of outrageous fun ahead when little girls get beautiful African American dolls Shani and her friends ready for their dancing debut on Soul Train! Each doll comes with glitter hair lotion for hours of hair stylin' fun! Shani and her friends Asha™ and Nichelle® wear the latest in hip hop fashion in ethnic prints. Jamal™ is Shani doll's boyfriend and her cool Soul Train dance partner! Girls will love the only African American teen dolls with attitude! For ages 3 years and over.

12¾"H x 6"W x 2½"D WINDOW BOX
10289 STD. PAK 6 (SHANI DOLL)
10290 STD. PAK 6 (NICHELLE DOLL)
10291 STD. PAK 6 (ASHA DOLL)
10288 STD. PAK 6 (JAMAL DOLL)

"Soul Train" and associated trademarks are owned by and used under license from Don Cornelius Productions, Inc. All Rights Reserved.

Each doll comes with glitter hair lotion.

Enjoy hours of hair stylin' fun!

10291 SOUL TRAIN ASHA Doll   10288 SOUL TRAIN JAMAL Doll   10289 SOUL TRAIN SHANI Doll   10290 SOUL TRAIN NICHELLE Doll

BEACH STREAK™ SHANI® DOLLS

Shani and her friends are cool African American dolls who combine beach fun and color-streaked hair play. Little girls will have hours of fun playing with their color-streaked hair. Their swimsuits are sure to stand out on the beach with their metallic accents and hot colors! Boyfriend Jamal™ wears a trendy black body tank with metallic accents, too! For ages 3 years and over.

12¾"H x 3½"W x 2½"D WINDOW BOX
3428 STD. PAK 6 (SHANI DOLL)
3457 STD. PAK 6 (ASHA™ DOLL)
3456 STD. PAK. 6 (NICHELLE® DOLL)
3802 STD. PAK 6 (JAMAL DOLL)

Have hours of fun playing with their color-streaked hair!

3802 JAMAL Doll   3457 ASHA Doll   3456 NICHELLE Doll   3428 SHANI Doll

SHANI® SIZZLING STYLE™ FASHIONS ASSORTMENT

Bold, gold style just for Shani and her friends. Three dramatic fashions to suit any occasion: stylish golden trench coat with scarf, casual ethnic print outfit and sophisticated black evening gown with golden jacket. Dolls not included. For ages 3 years and over.

12"H x 9"W BLISTER CARD
A5970 ASST. PAK 12

A5970 SHANI SIZZLING STYLE Fashions Assortment

5967   5968

The Shani dolls range, from the Mattel Girls' Toys Catalog, 1993.

1986–1998

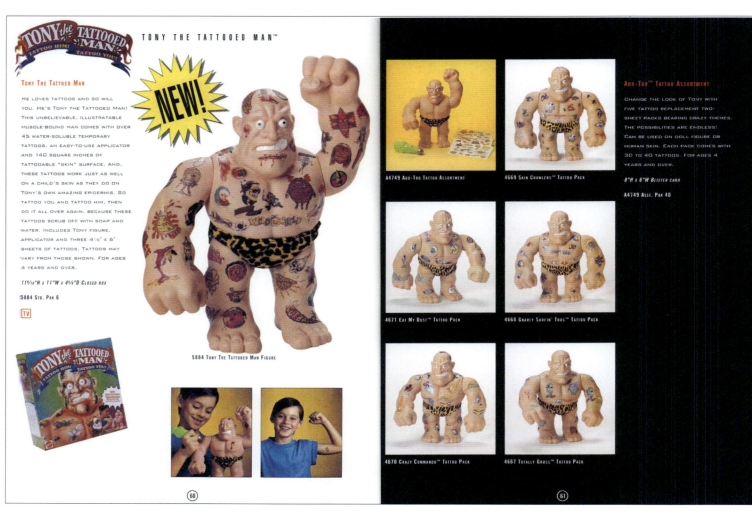

Tony the Tattooed Man and Streek X-Ploders, both from the Mattel Boys' Toys Catalog, 1993.

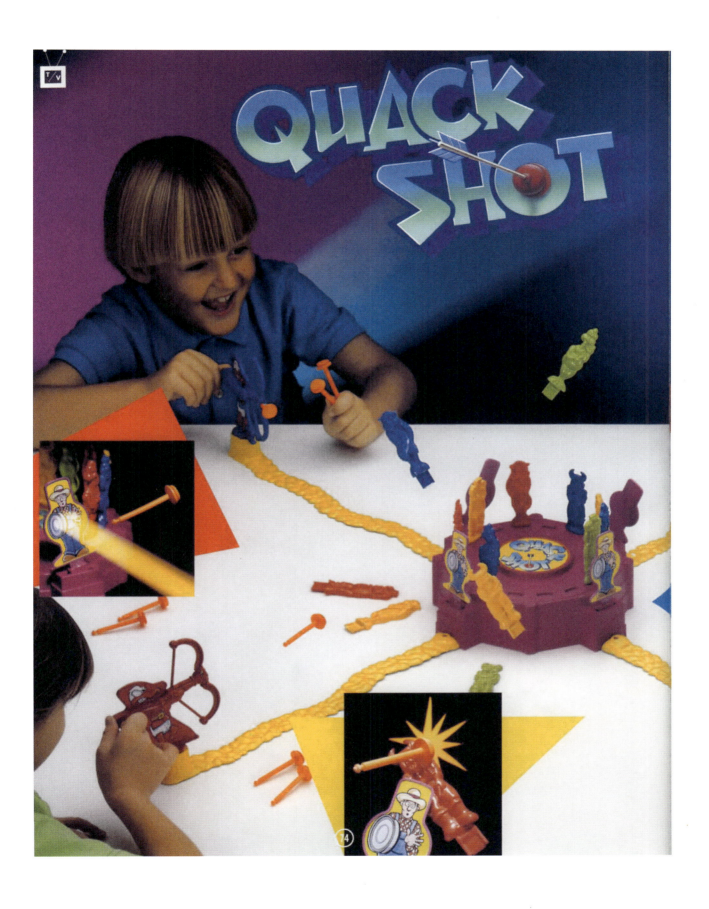

The Quack Shot game, from the Mattel Boys' Toys Catalog, 1993.

©1993 Nickelodeon. All Rights Reserved. Nickelodeon and all related characters are trademarks owned and licensed for use by Nickelodeon, a programming service of Viacom International Inc.

FLOAM

Build it! Shape it! Bounce it!
More possibilities than a bowl of day old oat[...]
Mold this colorful scrunchy substance wi[...]
your fingers in lots of different ways.
In 6 colors. Ages 3 and over.

A11436 Asst. Pak 24.
6" x 12" blister card.

ABOVE AND OPPOSITE: Floam and Gak, both introduced in the Mattel Boys' Games and Toys Catalog, 1994.

77081
Billy Blazes™,
Fire Fighter
Comes with
a chopping ax!

77082
Jack Hammer™,
Construction Expert
With action jackhammer!

Rescue Heroes™ Asst.

Ages 3 yrs. & up

These quick-response specialists are
equipped to save the day! Each figure
comes with a special tool and interchangeable equipment pack to make them ready
for rescue operations anytime, anywhere!

Ea. in blister card package. 7"l x 8.5"h x 4.5"d. 6 pcs. per 6.3 lb.
shipper (choice of assortment mix: 1 ea. of 77083 Scuba Diver and
77084 Mountain Ranger, and 2 ea. of 77081 Fire Fighter and 77082
Construction Expert; or 1 ea. of 77081 Fire Fighter and 77082
Construction Expert, and 2 ea. of 77083 Scuba Diver and 77084
Mountain Ranger).

New!

77083
Gil Gripper™,
Scuba Diver
His clamp
grabs and grips!
Removable
mask, too.

77084
Rocky Canyon™,
Mountain Ranger
With grappling hook that
shoots out! Thumb crank
reels hook back in.

ABOVE AND OPPOSITE: Rescue Heroes and Great Adventures sets, from the Fisher-Price Catalogs, 1998 and 1994 respectively.
FOLLOWING PAGES: Hot Wheels Treasure Hunt collectibles, from the Mattel Boys' Toys Catalog, 1995.

GREAT ADVENTURES

GREAT ADVENTURE CASTLE ▼
3 yrs. and up

Imagination reigns! Your little prince will conquer new worlds and defeat dark foes in countless fun-filled adventures. Small hands can easily work the flip-over catapult, tumbling tower and flip-down cannon for exciting, real-life action. Realistic castle features working drawbridge, kitchen and sleeping areas. Includes 8 moveable knights (complete with their own round table!) and 2 magic action kings.
Approx. retail price $44.00

Fisher-Price

NEW

...sh the king's own – the arm oves up and down.

Working catapult.

Working, flip down cannon.

Join the Fisher-Price® Family Registry

1•800•432•5437

- Hot Wheels® cars are hotter than ever--just look at what's new for '95!

- In addition to 12 new cars, we're also adding a special Treasure Hunt car each month to add to the excitement!

- Each sold separately. Some vehicles not for use with some sets. *Cars subject to change.

- For ages 3 and over.
A9890 Asst. Pak (A) 144
A9891 Asst. Pak (B) 144
6 1/2"H x 1 5/16"D x 4 1/4"W blister card.

Kids and adult collectors will be on the lookout for Treasure Hunt cars. This is a limited edition series of vehicles-only 10,000 produced each month.

13609 SPEED BLASTER*

13610 MERCEDES SL

13344 DODGE RAM Truck

13345 McLAREN F1*

13340 '94 CAMARO Convertible

13337 '58 CORVETTE

13341 SPEED-A-SAURUS™

13347 Snowmobile

13346 Power Racer

13348 Power Pistons

13342 Hydroplane

13339 VIPER Coupe*

CAMARO and CORVETTE are trademarks of General Motors Corporation and used under license to Mattel, Inc. FORD and MUSTANG trademarks used under license from Ford Motor Company. MERCEDES-BENZ trademarks used by permission.

10494 '32 FORD VICKY

10495 Deora

11524 Mutt Mobile

11522 S'Cool Bus

11523 Whip Creamer

10497 Snake

10783 Mongoose

10496 Custom MUSTANG

• Then and now, Hot Wheels® cars are always hot!

• Eight new cars for kids and collectors!

• Authentic replicas of the original Hot Wheels designs from 25 years ago!

• Each car features a limited edition color to increase its collectibility and value. These limited-run colors will change approximately once a month during production.

• To make them even more fun to collect, each Vintage Collection car comes with its own collector's button and serialized package!

• Each sold separately. Some vehicles not for use with some sets.

• For ages 3 and over.
A10509 Asst. Pak 72
5 7/8"H x 1 3/8"D x 5 3/4"W blister card.

7

UNO

UNO® Stacko™

- UNO® colors and numbers add a new dimension to the fun of a stacking game.
- Not only do players have to worry about steady hands, they also have to play by UNO® rules!
- Just like classic UNO®, UNO® Stacko is easy to learn and fun for the whole family.
- The roll of the UNO® cube helps to level the playing field, so anyone can be a winner.
- Gives loyal UNO® customers a new way to play.
- Includes 51 brightly colored UNO® blocks and one UNO® cube.
- For any number of players.
- Ages 8 and over.
- 9003 Std. Pak - 6
  3 ½" D x 3 ½" W x 12 ½"H closed box.

9003 UNO® STACKO™

UNO® Rummy-Up™

- Classic UNO® with a twist of rummy fun combined into one fast-paced, challenging game!
- Players match colorful game pieces using UNO® rules, then arrange them in sets of runs, rummy style!
- Players try to make a set with four tiles of the same number or make a run of four to 12 tiles in a sequence.
- Set includes 100 game tiles and four playing racks.
- For two to four players.
- Ages 7 to adult.
- 9002 Std. Pak - 6
  2 ½" D x 18 ¾" W x 9 ½" H closed box.

9002 UNO® RUMMY UP™

UNO® is a registered trademark of International Games, a Mattel Company.

9

UNO Stacko and UNO Rummy-Up, from the Mattel International Games Catalog, 1995.

UNO® is a registered trademark of International Games, a Mattel Company.

UNO was created in 1971 by Merle Robbins, a barber living in Reading, Ohio, who developed his own rules to the crazy eights card game to play with his family.

The game grew popular, and the Robbins family ultimately sold their home to raise enough money to print 5,000 copies of the game, which they named UNO after the rule they had added that players must announce when they were down to their last card, but also to market the game's name repeatedly—like bingo—during play. They sold the game out of Robbins's barber shop until they bought an old car and trailer and drove through the American Southeast selling the game, sporting signs on the sides that said, "UNO: The Best Game in America!"

UNO ultimately reached a national and global audience thanks to Bob Tezak, a funeral parlor owner and UNO superfan, who bought the rights to UNO and took the card deck worldwide, founding International Games Incorporated with a group of friends who all enjoyed the game. After selling through the last of Robbins's backstock, Tezak redesigned the cards, instructions, and packaging, and marketed the game across the country and abroad. Sales soared throughout the 1980s and early 1990s. Finally, in 1992, Tezak sold International Games Incorporated to Mattel.

BARBIE® FASHION AVENUE™ Assortment (Denim)

- Barbie doll's hottest, trendiest and most glamorous fashions, with lots of realistic details. Cool Trend, Denim, Outerwear and Short Glamour are part of a rolling mix which will be periodically refreshed. Each outfit has realistic details such as buttons and buckles.

  –14670 Denim overalls with attached hip pack, lace pink stretch top and beret.

  –14671 Denim skirt and jacket with fur-like trim and matching fur-like purse.

  –14672 Denim vest with white ruffled blouse, velvet-like shorts and high boots. (International only.)

  –14673 Denim short dress with "lace-up" detailing and sparkly golden jacket.

- Ages 3 and over. • 12"H x 7 1/2"W blister card.

FASHION AVENUE is a registered trademark of Newport News, a member of the Spiegel Group.

A14980 (DOMESTIC)
ASST. PAK 12
(PART OF ROLLING MIX)
UPC CODE: 74299-14980-1

A14364 (INTERNATIONAL)
ASST. PAK 12

22

Barbie Fashion Avenue dolls, from the Mattel Catalog, 1996.

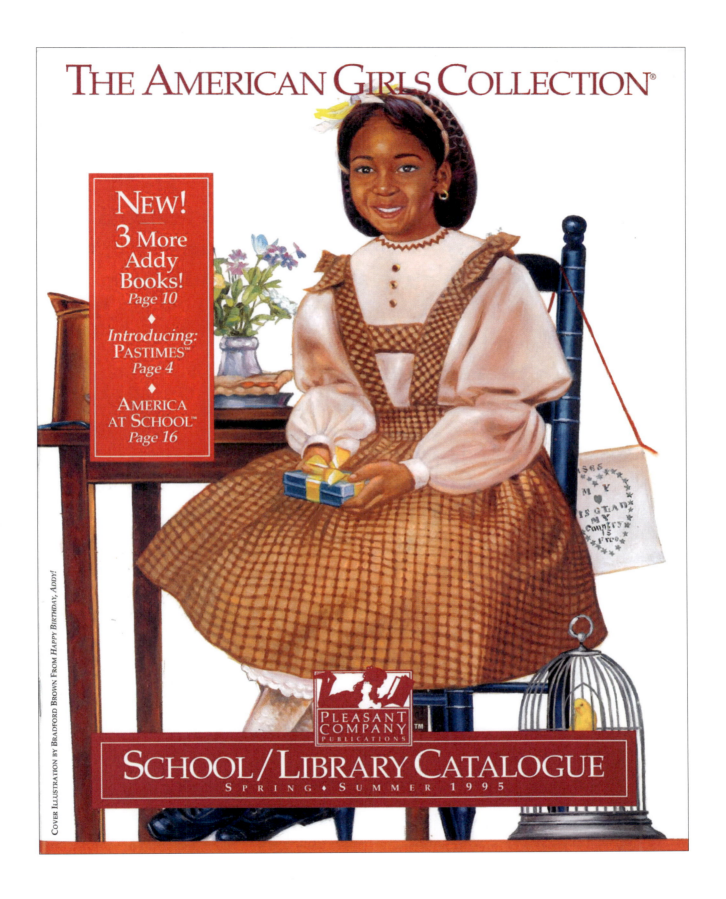

THE AMERICAN GIRLS COLLECTION®

NEW!
3 More Addy Books!
Page 10

◆

Introducing:
PASTIMES™
Page 4

◆

AMERICA AT SCHOOL™
Page 16

COVER ILLUSTRATION BY BRADFORD BROWN FROM *HAPPY BIRTHDAY, ADDY!*

PLEASANT COMPANY PUBLICATIONS™

SCHOOL/LIBRARY CATALOGUE
SPRING ◆ SUMMER 1995

ABOVE AND FOLLOWING PAGES: Cover and pages from the American Girls Collection School and Library Catalog, 1995.

Five Bright New **Boo**
Inspired by the favorite featur

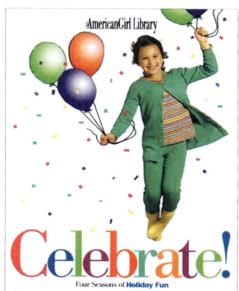

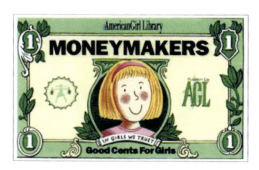

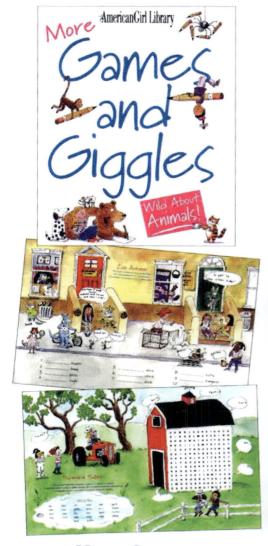

Celebrate!
Four Seasons of Holiday Fun

Crafts, games, recipes, party ideas, and more—a year's worth of special ways to give special days that clever *American Girl* touch. All major holidays are covered, as well as other occasions such as the first and last day of school. There are even ways to celebrate any day!

48 pages 1-56247-665-3 **$8.95**

Moneymakers
Good Cents for Girls

Girls love having their own money to spend—and save—as they wish. This book is full of moneymaking tips and ideas, advice from real girl entrepreneurs, and information on saving and spending. *Bonus extra:* business cards, price tags, and templates for other "business starters" to help a girl open her business right away!

64 pages 1-56247-668-8 **$7.95**

More Games and Giggles
Wild About Animals!

The sequel to our bestselling *Games and Giggles* has 96 more pages of tummy-tickling, brain-bending, side-splitting fun! Games, mazes, secret codes, and more—this time with an all-animal theme to keep American girls giggling!

96 pages 1-56247-664-5 **$5.95**

TO ORDER CALL
1-800-233-0264

First printing 120,000 of eac

for American Girls!

American Girl® magazine.

NEW
Super Slumber Party Kit
See order form for details

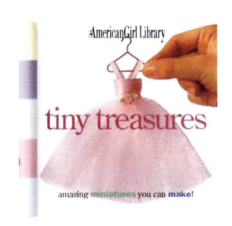

Each spread folds out to display step-by-step instructions.

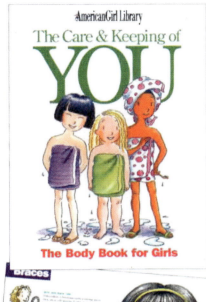

The Magazine Just for Girls!

American Girl, created especially for girls 8 and up, is one of the top-selling children's magazines in the country.

A Parent's Choice award winner, *American Girl* is a hit with readers and parents alike. Each issue is packed with fiction, games, puzzles, party plans, and more.

Available through Ingram Periodicals and other magazine wholesalers. Or direct from Pleasant Company in multiples of five. Nonreturnable.

Cover Price: **$3.95**
Published bimonthly

Tiny Treasures
Amazing Miniatures You Can Make!

This book shows girls how to turn everyday items into dozens of amazing miniatures. Make pies from bottle caps, plates from buttons, a table from balsa wood and golf tees! *Special feature:* a "little room" in the back of the book folds out to give girls a place to display and play with their tiny treasures.

86 pages 1-56247-667-X **$9.95**

The Care and Keeping of You
The Body Book for Girls

This engaging, informative, and age-appropriate guide answers all the questions preteen girls have about their bodies—from hair care to healthy eating, bad breath to bra buying, pimples to periods. *Note:* This book addresses preteen girls' concerns about basic health and hygiene. It does not address issues regarding human sexuality.

104 pages 1-56247-666-1 **$8.95**

Promotional Support

- National Consumer Advertising
- Titles promoted in 30 million catalogues mailed to consumers
- Co-op advertising available

tle—Available September!

19

Secret combs for
girls to find!

Ponies have real
mane and tails!

TV!

PONY PARADE COLLECTION™ Pony Compacts

• Polly Pocket® Pony Compacts have a delicate cameo pattern on the front plus all sorts of surprises inside. Polly's ponies have real mane and tails that girls can style with the hidden combs! Each compact also has a new double opening that extends the ponies' play area.

−14507 Shetland Pony Stables™: Articulated Polly has a pony with a saddle and blanket! The fence becomes a comb for the pony's hair. Inside the stable there's a secret loft that opens with a fold-out bed for Polly.

−14508 Palomino Pony™: Polly and her cat can ride around the manor house in a carriage pulled by her palomino pony. The front gate is really a comb to style the pony's hair! Inside the stable is a secret loft that opens for Polly.

−14509 Unicorn Meadow™: Polly dreamed she was a princess with a beautiful unicorn in a fantasy meadow. The top of the bench is really a comb! The tree trunk opens to reveal a bedroom for Polly.

• Ages 4 and over.   • 12 1/2"H x 6 1/2"W x 1 3/8"D blister card.

A15191 ASST. PAK 12
UPC CODE: 74299-15191-0

POLLY POCKET and associated characters and trademarks owned by Bluebird Toys (UK) Ltd., England. ©1995 Bluebird Toys (UK) Ltd.

KEEPSAKE COLLECTION™ Ring Assortment

- Little girls love collecting Polly Pocket® rings. They're fun to wear, and girls can play with them wherever they go! Each ring features a fun theme and comes with a removable Polly inside wearing a different hat. When the ring is closed, her hat pops out of the top to complete the decoration. Assortment includes:

  −14490 Crown Surprise™: Princess Polly loves to hide inside her royal crown on a pink cushion. Princess Polly's crown becomes part of the Crown Surprise!

  −14491 Pretty Egg Surprise™: Polly wears a crown that pops out of her decorative egg.

  −14492 Flower Surprise®: Flower Polly is hiding inside her beautiful bouquet of flowers! Inside, she stands on a bed of leaves and wears a beret that pops out of the flower.

  −14493 "Pearl" Pretty Surprise™: Mermaid Polly has a beautiful "pearl" hat that pops out of the shell. Inside, Polly stands on a bed of coral.

- Ages 4 and over. •6"H x 4"W x 1 1/8"D blister card.

A10619 ASST. PAK 12
UPC CODE: 74299-10619-4

POLLY POCKET and associated characters and trademarks owned by Bluebird Toys (UK) Ltd., England. ©1995 Bluebird Toys (UK) Ltd.

81

Polly Pocket was created in 1983 by Chris Wiggs, who, inspired by his daughter Kate's love for miniatures, fashioned a doll house out of an old yellow makeup powder compact, and filled it with teeny, tiny details and an even smaller doll to go with it.

Bluebird Toys in Swindon, England soon licensed the concept, tweaking the design to give Polly a hinged waist and releasing a small line of Polly Pocket playsets in stores by 1989, comprised of plastic cases that opened to form a house or play scene, and dolls that were less than one inch tall. In 1998 Mattel purchased Bluebird Toys, and finally acquired all rights to Polly Pocket from Wiggs in 2007.

Mattel introduced "Fashion Polly!" in 1999, a slightly bigger doll at 3.5" tall and with changeable rubber clothing, soon turning Polly into a multi-media star. In 2018, Mattel returned to the fun of the original-sized playsets and 3" dolls. The new sets inspired a wave of nostalgic merchandise including handbags, clothing, and makeup. A television series debuted in summer 2018 starring a girl named Polly whose magical locket allows her to shrink herself and her friends, currently in its 6th season.

OPPOSITE AND ABOVE: Polly Pocket compact and ring assortments, from the Bluebird Toys Catalog, 1995.

NEW

TV

• Dr. Piranoid™ wants to rule the world by turning ordinary sea creatures into "sea-viates"–twisted criminals intent on destruction. And only Ripster™ and his brothers can stop him!

• Inspired by the ultimate living predators, these big, buff sharks are always ready for a fight.

• Each articulated figure stands 6" tall, with an aggressive look and exciting action feature.

• Jab™, Ripster™, Blades™ and Big Slammu™ feature realistic shark skin.

• For ages 4 and over.
A12260 Asst. Pak 12
7 7/8"H x 4 1/16"D x 5 3/4"W
"try me" packaging.

JAB
• Heroic hammerhead shark is one mean customer, with arm-activated jackhammer punching and head-butting action.

RIPSTER
• Heroic great white shark boasts huge arms for a mighty, spring-activated roundhouse punch.

Turns into a piranha.

Snapping claws

12257 SLOBS

12259 DR. PIRANOID

12258 SLASH

Rotating screw-like nose.

Knockout punching.

Head-butting action.

12256 BIG SLAMMU

12253 JAB

12255 BLADES

12254 RIPSTER

Rolling skates, extending claws.

Roundhouse punching.

STREET SHARKS™

BLADES
• Heroic tiger shark rolls right into the thick of things, with working skates and extending hand claws.

BIG SLAMMU
• Heroic whale shark plays rough, with tree-trunk arms that deliver a spring-activated knockout punch.

SLOBSTER™
• Evil lobster has his own style of fighting. When his legs are squeezed, his claws snap and pinch.

SLASH™
• Evil swordfish skewers his victims with his rotating screw-like nose.

DR. PIRANOID
• Evil leader is the twisted mastermind behind a plot to take over the world. His head changes from human to piranha with the push of a lever. In a rumble, he relies on his spring-loaded harpoon.

©1994 Street Wise Designs, Inc. All Rights Reserved. STREET SHARKS™ is a trademark of Street Wise Designs, Inc. Exclusively licensed by Surge Entertainment, Inc.

1997 New Cars

- Mattel continues its tradition of excellence with great new cars for 1997.

- This year, Hot Wheels cars are even more collectible. There are 12 new four-car series, 12 1997 First Editions cars and 12 Treasure Hunt cars. Kids and adult collectors will want them all!

- Each car has incredible detail which has made Hot Wheels the leader in 1/64 scale cars for over 25 years.

- Each sold separately. Some vehicles not for use with some sets.

- Ages 3 and over.

- Blister card.

A3612 ASST. PAK (A) 72
UPC CODE: 74299-9890-1

A3612 ASST. PAK (B) 72
UPC CODE: 74299-9891-8

AURORA, CHEVY, CORVETTE, OLDS and 442 are trademarks of General Motors Corporation and used under license to Mattel, Inc. The Bull Device, the trademark AUTOMOBILI LAMBORGHINI, the trademark COUNTACH are owned by and used under license from Automobili Lamborghini S.P.A., Italy. AUDI trademarks used by permission. BMW trademarks used by permission. FORD trademark used under license from Ford Motor Company. HUMMER is a registered trademark of AM General Corporation, used under license. MERCEDES-BENZ trademarks used by permission. The NISSAN trademark and design are used by permission of Nissan North America, Inc.

148

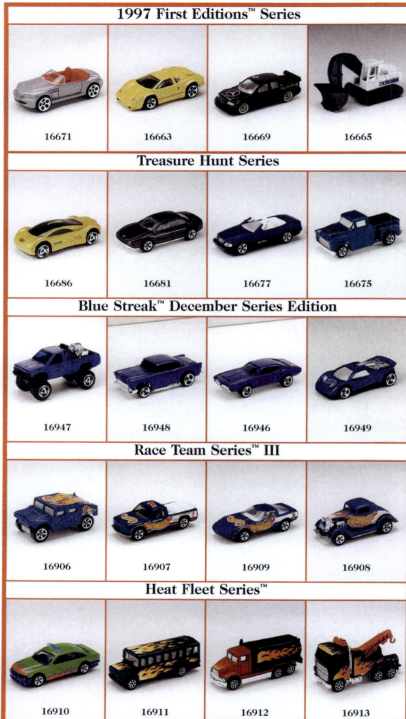

A3612 1997 New Series Assortment

The Matchbox 1–75 Collection, from the Tyco Catalog, 1997.

Compatibilit, from the Mattel Games and Puzzles Catalog, 1997.

Whatta Dump!, from the Mattel Games and Puzzles Catalog, 1997.

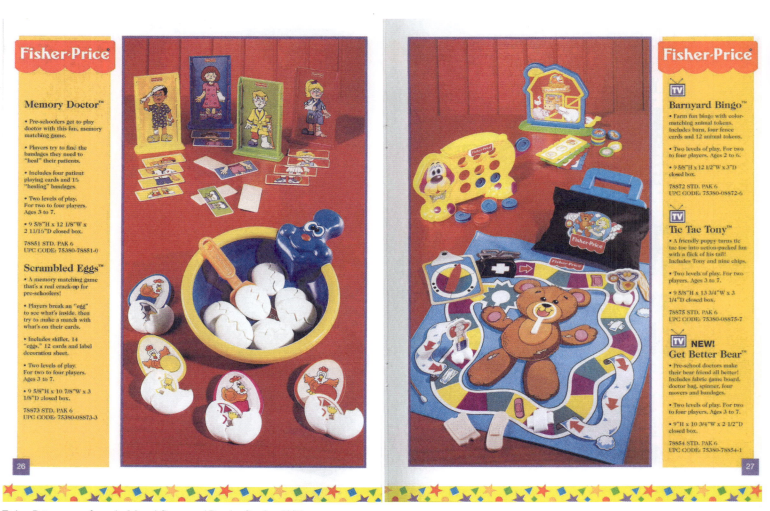

Fisher-Price games, from the Mattel Games and Puzzles Catalog, 1997.

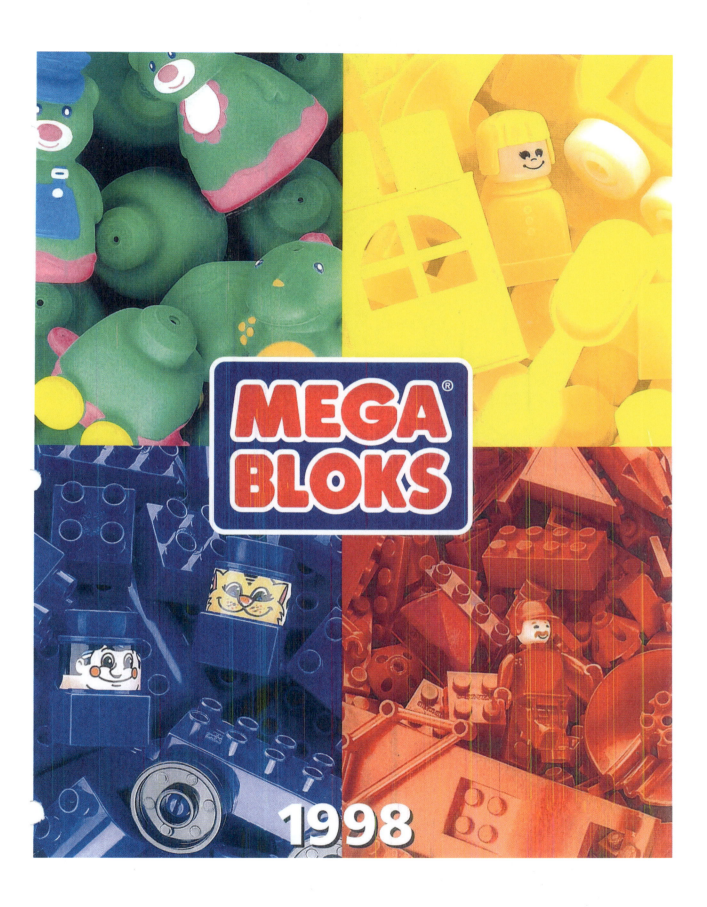

ABOVE: Cover of the Mega-Bloks catalog, 1998.
FOLLOWING PAGES: Tangerine Twist and Uptown Chic Barbie dolls, from the Mattel Barbie Collectibles Catalog, 1998.

TANGERINE TWIST

UP

TANGERINE TWIST™ BARBIE® DO

Meet the embodiment of today's sophisticated African-American woman in the new Fashon S Collection™ designed by African-American Bart designer, Kitty Black Perkins. The first in the series is Tangerine Twist. A dramatic, contemporary fashion in vibrant orange gives Barbie the look and feel of high fashion. Her long black hair is styled in a contemporary b cut and she has contemporary face paint and skin coloring. Her accessories include a faux leopard print hat, black leather like gloves an handbag and pumps. Also included is a labele doll stand, certificate of authenticity and reply card. For ages 14 and over.

13 1/2"H x 9"W x 3"D
Window Box
17860 Std. Pak 2

UPTOWN CHIC BARBIE® DOLL

Second in The Fashion Savvy Collection,™ a series that captures the unique image, style and sophistication of today's African-American woman, Uptown Chic Barbie is ablaze with vibrant color in a purely contemporary fashion. Her ensemble features a purple jumpsuit with a boldly striped "silk" wrap. Her dramatic accessories include a yellow wide brimmed hat with black trim, yellow shoulder bag, glasses, shoes and "cell phone". She wears her hair in a fashionably short style, has a fully poseable body and contemporary face paint and skin tone. Also included is a labeled doll stand, certificate of authenticity and reply card. For ages 14 and over.

13 1/2"H x 9"W x 3"D
Window Box
19632 Std. Pak 2

16

"*You're so* **scary** *cool.*"

CHAPTER FIVE

Making Moves in a New Millennium

As Mattel stepped into a new millennium, bigger and better than ever before, the company shifted focus back to its core brands. Mattel was committed to expanding Barbie, Hot Wheels, American Girl, and other favorite lines to provide more value for consumers and help those brands grow with children to inspire a lifelong love of play. Of course, acquisitions didn't stop entirely. Mattel purchased Radica Games in 2006, the game Apples to Apples in 2007, HiT entertainment in 2012, and Mega Bloks in 2014, all expansions that helped support and provide collaboration opportunities for Mattel's core brands.

1999–2014

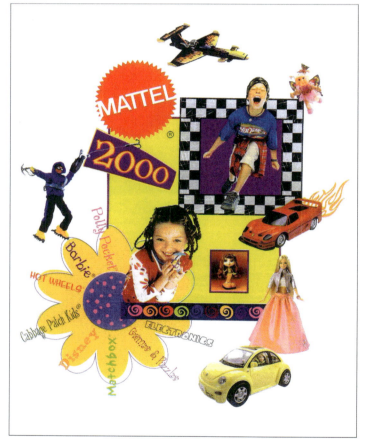

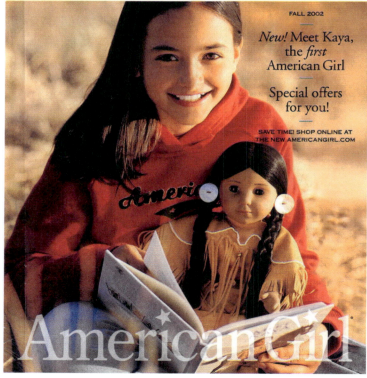

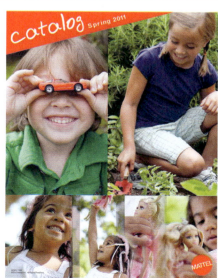

Mattel had seen firsthand how American Girl had grown beyond dolls to become a lifestyle brand for young girls thanks to store experiences, books, and fashions. Mattel opened additional American Girl stores across the country and partnered with Julia Roberts' Red Om films to produce a line of movies about their most popular characters. They also expanded the doll offerings available, adding a Girl of the Year doll starting in 2001. These limited-edition dolls allowed American Girl to feature contemporary characters and stories alongside their traditional historical options.

On the Hot Wheels side, Mattel leaned into what its fans loved best about the brand: cool, exclusive cars. In 2001, a life-sized replica of popular Hot Wheels racer the Twin Mill debuted at an auto show in Vegas. That same year, Mattel launched a Hot Wheels collectors' website to connect with avid fans both young and old. In 2005, Mattel released its Hot Wheels Classic Line, focusing on muscles cars and hot rods, many from the first decade of Hot Wheels production, much to the delight of car enthusiasts. At the same time, Hot Wheels also prioritized partnering with leading OEMs to create an all-encompassing line catering to all facets of adult automotive enthusiasts.

Barbie reached new levels of high fashion with a cover for Italian Vogue as part of the Black Issue, which celebrated 30 years since the first Black Barbie was introduced in 1980. Mattel also released the So In Style line of Black Barbies with different skin tones; more authentic-looking facial features; and curlier hair, developed and inspired by Barbie designer Stacey McBride-Irby, a Black mother of two who wanted to create a line of dolls more reflective of her daughter and community.

While Barbie continued to inspire millions of consumers, in 2010 Mattel packaging designer Garrett Sander noticed a shift in girls gravitating toward darker, edgier fashion. He thought Mattel needed a doll line with a dark aesthetic that complemented the Barbie brand; so, the team decided to create a new line of dolls based on classic monsters like vampires, werewolves, and mummies. Monster High launched with a line of dolls, clothes, and accessories; a YouTube series; a line of young adult books by bestselling author Lisi Harrison; and animated specials for TV. It was the biggest hit for an original Mattel toy line since Masters of the Universe. That success served as a good reminder for everyone at Mattel that, while acquisitions continued to prove a sure source for growth, a good portion of Mattel's best concepts originated from within the company itself.

235

OPPOSITE, CLOCKWISE FROM UPPER LEFT: Covers from The American Girl Collection, 2001; Mattel Catalogs, 2001 and Fall 2014; American Girl Catalog, 2002; Mattel Catalogs, Spring 2011 and 2000.

Catalog Archive

1999

MATTEL

Cover of the Mattel Catalog, 1999.

Fashion Polly!

Polly can dress up for the first time ever! New Fashion Polly is a 3 1/2" doll that comes with lots of cool fashions and accessories. Dress her for any adventure!

Beach Time Fun Playset
Polly is ready for fun in the sun, with clothes that take her from the surf, to the sand, to beach party land! Includes Polly, three swimsuits, wetsuit, jogging outfit and three party outfits.
•From the Fashion Polly Doll assortment A23555.
•Peggable box.
•Ages 4 and over.
•TV
22020 STD. PAK 6

School Time Fun Playset
Polly's the most popular girl in school, with cool clothes that take her from class, to the track, to the school dance and back! Includes Polly, three prom dresses, track outfit, cheerleading outfit and three mix-and-match outfits for class.
•From the Fashion Polly Doll assortment A23555.
•Peggable box.
•Ages 4 and over.
•TV
22021 STD. PAK 6

ABOVE AND OPPOSITE: Polly Pocket accessories and Dreambuilders set, from the Mattel Catalog, 1999.

Dreambuilders

Design and redesign Polly's Dream House! Each room is stackable, open and closed. Collect all the rooms and build the biggest house on the block.

Bedroom

Mix and match rooms from the Collector Room Assortment and the Deluxe Mansion to build your own special dreamhouse!

Disco

Nursery

Art Studio

Collector Room Assortment

Four different collectible double rooms with lots of movable parts and tiny surprises.
Assortment includes:
23166 Nursery
23164 Art Studio
23163 Disco
23165 Bedroom
•Blister Card
•TV
A23171 ASST. PAK 12

FOLLOWING PAGES: The 40th Anniversary Barbie, from the Mattel Barbie Collectibles Catalog, 1999.

40th

CELEBRATING FORTY YEARS OF DREAMS

40 Barbie

Who, but Barbie, could look even better on h
40th anniversary than on her first debut? It's
wonder that this inimitable fashion doll is the
most collectible in the world. 1959 meets 19
as Barbie® doll dons a black flock bodice
shimmering with silvery glitter nostalgically
reminiscent of her original 1959 striped-patte
bathing suit. 40th Anniversary Barbie® doll is
stunning in her slim silhouette gown of black
organza that spills to a delicate tulip hemline
An illusion neckline of sheer black and daring
dangly earrings offset her soft French twist a
exquisitely charming face. Adding a dynamic
touch to celebrate her 40th anniversary is a
bountiful bouquet of 40 pink "roses," she
gracefully holds in her arms covered with she
black opera-length gloves. To complete the l
a miniature replica of the original 1959 doll a
package are included. Original then, original
the 40th Anniversary Barbie® doll is a must h
for seasoned collectors as well as anyone wh
wants to begin a Barbie collection with the d
that marks the new millennium.
For ages 14 and over.

13 1/2"H x 3"W x 10"D
Open Window Box
21384 (White) Std Pak 2
22336 (Black) Std Pak 2

A miniature replica of
the original 1959 doll
and package.

Anniversary

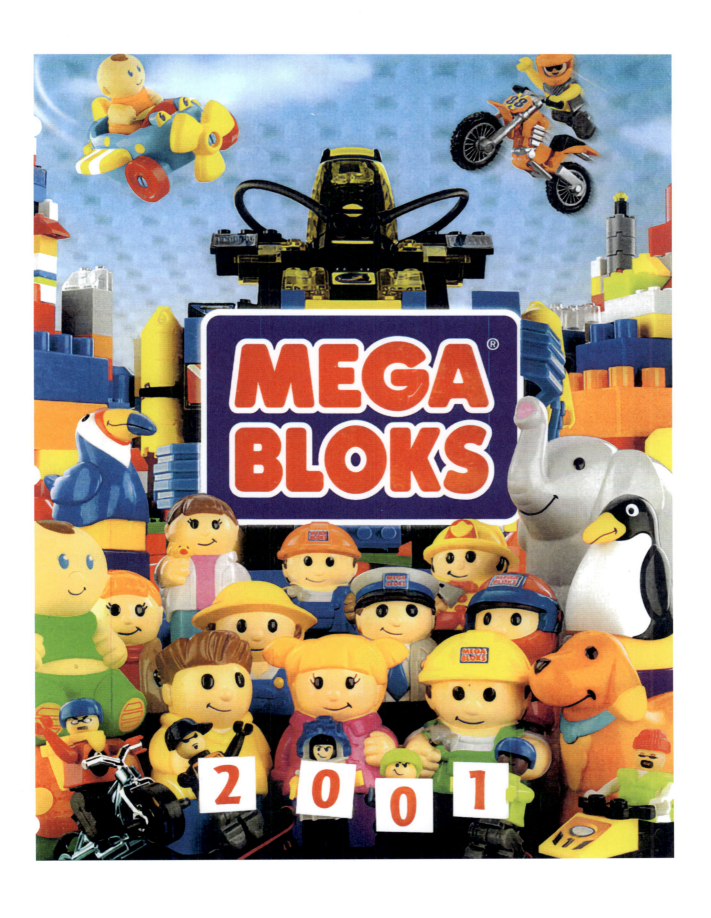

The Mega Bloks Catalog, 2001.

Extra Track

A whole new way to package, merchandise and sell Hot Wheels® open stock track – 120 pieces of 21" Hot Wheels® orange, low wall track with connectors attached.

- Not for use with some Hot Wheels vehicles and sets.
- Box with header.
- Ages 5 and over.
- TV

A21026 STD. PAK 1

Tune-up Shop

Kids can now service and repair their 1/64-scale Hot Wheels® cars. Features include a sparking mechanism, movable oil canister, elevator and dynamometer/revving mechanism that launches cars out of the service area.

- Vehicles not included.
- Not for use with some Hot Wheels vehicles.
- Closed box.
- Ages 5 and over.
- TV

21529 ASST. PAK 3

ABOVE AND OPPOSITE: Hot Wheels Tune-Up Shop and track sets, from the Mattel Catalog, 1999.

Hot Wheels® Racing X-V Racers™ Cars

NASCAR® and F1 replicas with rechargeable motors inside for authentic race day action and excitement at home!
- Charger included.
- Batteries not included.
- Not for use with some Hot Wheels sets.
- Blister card.
- Ages 5 and over.
- TV

23031 ASST. PAK 12

X-V Racers™ Scorcher Chamber™ Stunt Set

A unique stunt track set that highlights the features of Light Speeders™ vehicles. Kids can race, pass and crash, then turn out the lights for even more amazing racing action!
- Not for use with some Hot Wheels® vehicles.
- Requires three "AA" batteries, not included.
- Closed box.
- Ages 5 and over.
- TV

21428 STD. PAK 6

Race in the dark!

FOLLOWING PAGES: The Hot Wheels Monster Trucks range, from the Mattel Catalog, 2000.

Deluxe Grave Digger Truck*

A large scale monster truck that "comes to life" with flashing lights and cool engine sounds. Kids can make it drive straight or perform "wheelies." For exciting stunt action, kids can make the truck climb a wall, then do an outrageous flip! The truck has high and low gears and makes different engine sounds for each gear.

- Not for use with Hot Wheels® sets.
- Batteries not included.
- "Try me" open box.
- Ages 3 and over.
- TV

*Name subject to change.
Direct import.
88173 STD. PAK 1

Hot Wheels® Monster Jam*

Combines two of boys' favorites monster trucks and pro wrestling a cool new collection of Hot Whe 1/64 scale die-cast vehicles! The mean machines have four-whee turning, heavy-duty rubber tires the toughest drivers around. The assortment includes Grave Digge King Krunch, WCW Nitro Machin Sting, Hogan and Goldberg.

- Not for use with Hot Wheels
- Blister card.
- Ages 3 and over.
- TV

*Name subject to change.
A21572 ASST. PAK 6

Monster Trucks

A collection of six big, bad monster trucks, with distinctive Hot Wheels® styling. These heavy-duty, off-road vehicles are friction powered, with cool rumbling and shaking features. Each truck is approximately 4.5" long, with a chrome-like grille and oversized tires. The assortment includes Bigfoot Super Duty, Gunslinger, Sampson, Bearfoot, Black Stallion and Virginia Giant.

- Not for use with Hot Wheels sets.
- Window box.
- Ages 3 and over.
- TV

Direct import.
A89853 ASST. PAK 6

MONSTER TRUCKS

Generation Girl™ Dolls

The Generation Girl™ friends are ready for the International High dance party! They're looking cooler than ever with trendy party fashions and realistic accessories that further develop their distinct personalities and interests. Generation Girl includes six cool friends–Tori™ doll, Barbie® doll, Nichelle® doll and Lara™ doll, plus two new friends, Blaine™ doll and Mari™ doll. Tori, the extreme sports buff, comes with snowboarding gear. Barbie, the photographer, comes with photography accessories. Nichelle, the aspiring model, has hair and makeup accessories. Lara, the trendy artist, has drawing and sketching supplies. Blaine, the DJ, has the ultimate DJ equipment. Mari, the technology buff from Japan, comes with electronic games and gadgets. Each doll comes with an extra fashion, doll stand and the Generation Beat™ magazine.

• Window box.

• Ages 6 and over.

• TV

25766 (BARBIE®) STD. PAK 6
25767 (NICHELLE®) STD. PK 6
25768 (TORI™) STD. PAK 6
25769 (LARA™) STD. PAK 6
26111 (BLAINE™) STD. PAK 6
26112 (MARI™) STD. PAK 6

21

Generation Girl dolls, from the Mattel Catalog, 2000.

Jam 'N Glam™ Barbie® Dolls

Barbie®, Christie® and Teresa® dolls are cool rockers with trendy looks on stage and off. Each doll also has a fun hairstyle that flips to an outrageous color. Girls will love getting Barbie doll ready for the show by transforming her clothes, turning her hair purple, adding hair extensions and slipping on her headset. Dolls also have the twisty Ever-Flex™ waist. Now Barbie doll's ready to perform in the Jam 'n Glam Tour Bus™! Each doll comes with an on-stage look, off-stage look, three hair extensions, headset, sunglasses, two CDs and a poster.

- Window box.
- Ages 3 and over.
- TV

50257 (BARBIE®) STD. PAK 6
UPC CODE: 74299-50257-6
50258 (CHRISTIE®) STD. PAK 6
UPC CODE: 74299-50258-3
50259 (TERESA®) STD. PAK 6
UPC CODE: 74299-50259-0

11

Jam 'n' Glam Barbie dolls, from the Mattel Catalog, 2001.

![Barbie Nutcracker logo]

Sugarplum Princess Barbie® and Ken® as Prince Eric Dolls

Barbie® doll and Ken® doll let girls play out beauty and romance of Barbie doll's first feat length movie, "Barbie in the Nutcracker™," w magical transformations and fun dancing feat Barbie transforms from a ballerina into a prin and Ken transforms from a nutcracker into a prince. When girls put them on Barbie doll's special stand, Barbie and Ken can dance together just like in the movie.

• Window box.

• Ages 3 and over.

50792 (BARBIE® CAUCASIAN) STD. PAK 6
UPC CODE: 74299-50792-2

52690 (BARBIE® AFRICAN-AMERICAN) STD. PA
UPC CODE: 74299-52690-9

50793 (KEN® CAUCASIAN) STD. PAK 6
UPC CODE: 74299-50793-9

52689 (KEN® AFRICAN-AMERICAN) STD. PAK 6
UPC CODE: 74299-52689-3

Barbie® in The Nutcracker Marzipan and the Candy Sleigh

Girls will love re-creating their favorite scenes from the feature length movie, "Barbie and the Nutcracker™." This beautiful candy-inspired carriage looks like the one in the movie, sparkling with "candy jewels." Girls will love combing the horse's long, beautiful hair and decorating it with the pretty pink hair ribbon barrettes.

• Closed box.

• Dolls not included.

• Ages 3 and over.

50309 STD. PAK 4
UPC CODE: 74299-50309-2

Nutcracker Kelly® Assortment

Girls will love playing out the whole magical story of "Barbie in the Nutcracker™" with Kelly® doll and her friends. Each of these adorable dolls has a stand that snaps into Barbie's dance stand (sold separately), so the dolls can really dance just like in the movie.

The assortment includes:
- –50794 Tommy® doll as Gingerbread Boy
- –50795 Kelly® doll as Snow Fairy
- –50796 Tommy® doll as Major Mint
- –50797 Jenny® doll as Flower Fairy
- –50798 Kelly® doll as Peppermint Girl
- –50799 Tommy® doll as Colonel Candy

- Window box.
- Ages 3 and over.

A50682 ASST. PAK 12
UPC CODE: 74299-50682-6

1999–2014

27

OPPOSITE AND ABOVE: The Nutcracker Barbie range, from the Mattel Catalog, 2001.
FOLLOWING PAGES: UNO games and accessories, from the Mattel Catalog, 2000.

UNO Stacko™ Refresh

Redesigned to play more like UNO, the #1 card game! Great family entertainment that combines the fun of UNO with the challenge of Stacko. This refreshed version is just like UNO, with commands on the tiles themselves that include Wild, Reverse, Draw 2 and Skip.
• Closed box.
• Ages 8 and over.
42468 STD. PAK 4

UNO® Attack!™ Card Game

Now the #1 family card game is even faster and more unpredictable! Instead of drawing cards from a deck, players receive a random number of cards from the automatic card dispenser. There are also new command cards that give players different strategic options.
• Batteries not included.
• Window box.
• Ages 6 and over.
• TV
41943 STD. PAK 4

UNO Blitzo™

A fast, fun, electronic, table-top version of UNO for up to four players! Each player has four "card" buttons, each with a color and a number. A sliding "pass" switch allows players to pass play to the left or right. The game gives verbal cues, telling players what colors and/or numbers are being played. There are four different levels of difficulty.
• Clamshell blister.
• Ages 7 and over.
42458 STD. PAK 4

UNO® Card Game

America's #1 Family Game is as popular as ever! Easy to play, so the whole family can have fun together. For two to ten players, individual or team play.
• Ages 7 and over.
41001 (BLISTER CARD)
42001 (DISPLAY)

163

75 Collection

Unique die-cast vehicles with real heroic power! This collection offers kids real-life vehicle play patterns, including 35 new models for 2001. Themes include fire, police, construction, sports cars and more.

- Blister card.
- Ages 3 and over.

A30782 ASST. PAK 72
UPC CODE: 35995-30782-7

75 COLLECTION

5-car Gift Packs

Each set features a different parent-friendly theme that appeals to kids and encourages collecting. The assortment features themes such as rescue and adventure, including 12 new themes for 2001. Each 1/64 vehicle is incredibly detailed, with a die-cast body and realistic tires.

- Window box.
- Ages 3 and over.

A30332 ASST. PAK 12
UPC CODE: 35995-30332-4

GIFT PACKS

10-car Gift Sets and Rescue Launcher Packs

This assortment includes 10 themed vehicle sets and rescue launcher packs, including 35 new models for 2001. The 1/64 scale die-cast vehicles feature fun themes such as fire, police and rescue. Many of the vehicles have moving parts, like extending ladders, opening doors, turning propellers and tipping truck beds.

Tray in box.

Ages 3 and over.

34307 ASST. PAK 6
UPC CODE: 35995-34307-8

Sky Busters® Planes

Realistic, highly detailed die-cast airplanes that look just like the real thing! Kids will love collecting all of their favorites. The assortment includes contemporary military and commercial planes with authentic decorations, plus fun licenses.

- Blister card.
- Ages 3 and over.
- Direct import.

A68982-80 ASST. PAK 36
UPC CODE: 35995-68982-0

GIFT SETS

SKY BUSTERS®

POWER WHEELS by Fisher-Price®

THE ELIMINATOR

New!

73180
The Eliminator™
Exciting lights and sounds put this baby right in the fast lane for fun! It's got an easy flip-down door, roomy cockpit with adjustable seat, working shifter, and cool "chrome-like" detailing. Kids can press the lights and sounds bar for cool robotic voices, special sound effects and flashing lights. Requires 3 "AA" alkaline batteries for sound.
Ages 3+
Maximum weight: 65 lbs. (30 kg)
Shipper/Individual
U.S. Patents D410,258; 4,555,451; 4,558,263; 5,644,114; 5,931,524 & patent pending.

Vehicle Specifications

12V RECHARGEABLE SYSTEM
BATTERY & CHARGER INCLUDED
HARD SURFACES & GRASS
MAXIMUM SPEED: **2.5 & 5 MPH** FORWARD
2.5 MPH REVERSE
SINGLE PEDAL OPERATION & POWER LOCK®
BRAKE FOR AUTOMATIC STOPS

Exciting lights and sounds!

Pull-down door for easy in and out.

120

PREVIOUS PAGES: The Matchbox 75 Collection cars and Sky Busters planes, from the Mattel Catalog, 2001.
ABOVE: The Power-Wheels Eliminator, from the Fisher-Price Catalog, 2001.

ONE YEAR
1
BUMPER TO BUMPER
WARRANTY
(BATTERIES EXCLUDED - SEE DETAILS)

ONE YEAR
BUMPER-TO-BUMPER
WARRANTY

Limited one-year warranty
for all Power Wheels®
ride-on toy vehicles.
Six-month limited warranty
on batteries included with
the original purchase of the
Power Wheels® vehicles.

ELIMINATOR

257

1999–2014

121

• KIRSTEN 1854 • ADDY 1864 • SAMANTHA 1904 • KIT 1934 • MOLLY 1944 • KAYA 1764 • FELICITY 1774 • JOSEFINA 1824 • KIRSTEN 1854 • ADDY 18

The AMERICAN GIRLS COLLECTION™

Do you love to curl up with a good book? Do you dream of having a doll so beautiful you'll cherish her for years to come?

The American Girls Collection® introduces you to a growing group of girls who lived in exciting times in the past. Like you and your friends, each one is unique. As you read their stories and bring them to life with your dolls, you'll see that some things in their lives were very different from yours. But you'll also discover that family, friendship,

MEET ADDY *An American Girl*

MEET SAMA

MEET KAYA *An American Girl*

MEET FELIC *An American*

Celebrate the timele

New!
Kaya—adventurous

Felicity—spunky

Josefina—hopeful

Kirsten—strong

*Find Felicity at
americangirl.com*

and feelings meant just as much to them as they do to you. It's these important things that connect you with girls from long ago, and remind you of what makes being a girl great!

All the dolls in The American Girls Collection are keepsake quality, designed to last through hundreds of hugs and years of play. They're 18 inches tall and have soft bodies with arms and legs you can pose. Their sparkly eyes open and close and their thick, beautiful hair is fun to brush and style.

Turn the page to meet the American Girls, or see them at americangirl.com!

aditions of girlhood

Addy—courageous

Samantha—kind

Kit—resourceful

Molly—a dreamer

259

1999–2014

5

The American Girls Collection, from the American Girl Catalog, Fall 2002.

What makes an American Girl Today?

Spirit and style, independence and imagination. A one-of-a-kind mind and an original point of view. A story to tell that's all her own.

You've asked to read about American Girls of today. Now, we're bringing them to you— each year, a great new girl with her own story!

Lindsey's an American Girl Today...

Lindsey Bergman™ is laugh-out-loud funny, with a brain for big ideas and a passion for principles. Her heart is always in the right place...but the rest of her is usually in trouble!

...but she's only here for one year!

Lindsey is available only for a limited time. Next year we'll introduce a new American Girl Today with her own personality and point of view!

Limited quantities available until December 31, 2002, or while supplies last.

American Girl
TODAY

Lindsey
by Chryssa Atkinson

Lindsey gets around town on a shiny silver **scooter**...except when it gets taken away as a punishment! Lindsey's **gloves** help her hold on to the handles as she flies down the sidewalk. Don't forget her butterfly **helmet** in case she slips off!
B9-GBK $34

w! Lindsey Doll & Book

Your Lindsey™ doll has curly auburn hair and bright blue eyes that open and close. She arrives dressed in a sporty green T-shirt and a khaki skirt. Her hooded **sweater** has contrasting stripes at the cuffs that match her colorful striped **tights**. Lindsey wears red ankle **boots** and a beaded **bobby** pin to hold back her bangs. She comes with a *Lindsey* paperback book.
39-GT2002 $84
Available until December 31, 2002, or while supplies last.

w! Lindsey Book

In *Lindsey,* you'll meet Lindsey Bergman, a funny, good-hearted ten-year-old girl who just can't help wanting to...well, *help!* She's trying to turn her teachers into lovebirds, keep her school safe from bullies, plan her brother's bar mitzvah, get her grumpy uncle to smile, and find her lost dog—all at once. But sometimes her best intentions bring more trouble than success!
Paperback Book B9-54502 $6.95

new! Laptop & Bag

Lindsey doesn't go anywhere without her **laptop**. Best of all, it keeps you *both* connected! Store 50 names and phone numbers, view the date and time, and use the calculator while you're out and about. Two pretend mini **disks** slide into the side of the laptop. Lindsey can carry her laptop along with her **notebook** and **pencil** in her messenger-style **computer** bag.
B9-GSAC2 $32 *Laptop requires 2 button-cell batteries, included.*

Use Lindsey's laptop as your own **personal organizer!**

Lindsey's collection

Lindsey Doll & Book, Scooter, plus Laptop & Bag
B9-GT2002S $135 save $15!

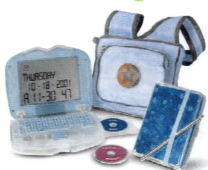

The introduction of Lindsey Bergman, from the American Girls Catalog, Fall 2001.

Valentine MAGIC 8 BALL® Novelty Toy
Let the Valentine Magic 8 Ball® be yours! This love-themed Magic 8 Ball® has all the answers for Valentine's Day gift giving. With 20 Valentine-themed answers, it's the perfect way to celebrate Cupid's favorite holiday. Ages 6 and over.
R9735 STD. PAK 6
UPC CODE: 027084-66217-1

Halloween MAGIC 8 BALL® Novelty Toy
This spook-tacular Magic 8 Ball® novelty toy has Halloween-themed answers to all of your most haunting questions. Ages 6 and over.
N5877 STD. PAK 6
UPC CODE: 027084-68327-1

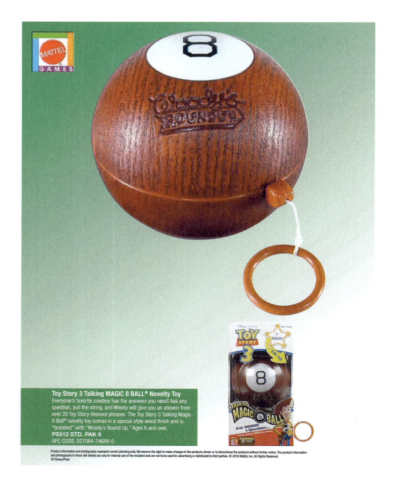

Toy Story 3 Talking MAGIC 8 BALL® Novelty Toy
Everyone's favorite cowboy has the answers you need! Ask any question, pull the string, and Woody will give you an answer from over 20 Toy Story-themed phrases. The Toy Story 3 Talking Magic 8 Ball® novelty toy comes in a special style wood finish and is "branded" with "Woody's Round Up." Ages 6 and over.
P5312 STD. PAK 6
UPC CODE: 027084-74699-0

CraZ 4 TXT™ MAGIC 8 BALL® Novelty Toy
The CraZ 4 Txt™ Magic 8 Ball® novelty toy has the answers to all your most texting needs! Ask any question on any matter, turn over the CraZ 4 Txt™ Magic 8 Ball® and you'll get the answer in the form of a text message! Ages 6 and over.
R4631 STD. PAK 6
UPC CODE: 027084-82351-6

Magic 8-Balls, from the Mattel Boys' Toys Catalog, 2010.

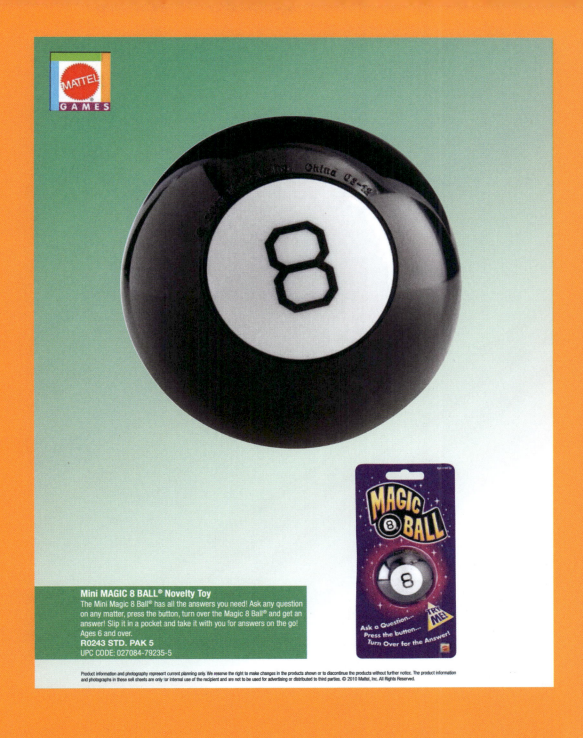

Mini MAGIC 8 BALL® Novelty Toy
The Mini Magic 8 Ball® has all the answers you need! Ask any question on any matter, press the button, turn over the Magic 8 Ball® and get an answer! Slip it in a pocket and take it with you for answers on the go! Ages 6 and over.
R0243 STD. PAK 5
UPC CODE: 027084-79235-5

Product information and photography represent current planning only. We reserve the right to make changes in the products shown or to discontinue the products without further notice. The product information and photographs in these sell sheets are only for internal use of the recipient and are not to be used for advertising or distributed to third parties. © 2010 Mattel, Inc. All Rights Reserved.

The original Magic 8 Ball component was invented in 1946 by Albert C. Carter in Cincinnati, Ohio, inspired by a spirit writing device used by his mother, who styled herself as a clairvoyant. Her device was a chalk slate inside of a closed container, which inspired Albert and his business partners Max Levinson and Abe Bookman—together Alabe Crafts, Inc—to create several iterations of similar ideas for his mother until, in 1948, Bookman hit on the design that, then named the Syco-Seer, would ultimately become the Magic 8 Ball. Inspired by crystal balls used in psychic readings, Bookman changed the shape from a cylinder to a sphere with a flat-sided window. Once Brunswick Billiards in Chicago used the design as a marketing tool in 1950, the Syco-Seer became the Magic 8 Ball from that point forward.

In 1971, Ideal Toys acquired Alabe Crafts and marketed the Magic 8 Ball to children, who loved the toy. In 1989, Tyco Toys purchased the rights to the toy and launched a new marketing campaign that drove up sales and renewed interest. Then, in 1997, Mattel purchased Tyco and, with it, the rights to the Magic 8 Ball.

HOT WHEELS® T-WRECKS™ PLAYSET

The Hot Wheels® T-Wrecks™ playset is where kids have the power to battle and destroy a gigantic T-Rex! The T-Rex "eats" and spits out cars, kids knock the captive car right out of his jaws! There is a kid-controlled attack ramp to launch cars and a motorized booster to shoot cars up the T-Rex's back. Includes cool electronic sound effects and other features for exciting play action.
• Closed box. • Ages 4 and over.
• Requires two "D" batteries, not included.

57439 STD. PAK 2
UPC CODE: 74299-57439-9

ALIEN ATTACK™ PLAYSET

Kids control a car-smashing alien with surprise action features, awesome electronic sound effects and a car vortex trap. Can you get past the alien before he catches you? The alien claw is triggered by the vehicle and the alien leaps out of the set to "catch" the car. Includes a robotic arm to hoist car to the top of the space station and a rotating car scanner!
• Closed box. • Ages 4 and over.
• Unassembled. • Not for use with some Hot Wheels® vehicles. • Two "AA" batteries required, not included. • TV

57438 STD. PAK 4
UPC CODE: 74299-57438-2

TRO CITY POLICE FORCE

CLIFF RACE

PLAYSET ASSORTMENT

These two sets deliver tons of action and unexpected surprises that kids love! Cliff Race lets kids race their car down the jagged cliff face and blast through the mountain wall. With the Metro City Police Force kids play out a high-speed pursuit through city streets smashing through a breakaway brick wall. Includes one exclusively decorated Hot Wheels® car.
• Window box. • Ages 3 and over. • Not for use with some Hot Wheels® sets.
• Direct import.
A88437 ASST. PAK 6
UPC CODE: 74299-88437-5

Bring learning to life!

Fisher-Price

Now I know my A-B-C's...

New!

Teaches:
- *Letters A – Z*
- *Numbers 1 – 10*
- *Shapes, music & more!*

Toby sings three fun learning songs!

Toby the Totbot

Now toddlers can discover just how much fun learning can be, with Toby the Totbot – a special little learning friend all their own. Toby's friendly voice and light-up display screen helps toddlers learn the alphabet, numbers, and shapes the way they learn best – through singing, dancing and lots of interactive fun. Approx. 11"H. Requires 3 "C" batteries.
Ages 1 year & up F3-PC0438 . . . . . $20.00

Available at toy stores everywhere!

266

1999–2014

6

PREVIOUS PAGES: Hot Wheels T-Wrecks and Alien Attack playsets, from the Mattel Catalog, 2003.

Kasey the Kinderbot

Great job! Give me five!

Kasey the Kinderbot™ Learning System

Kids will have fun learning the ABCs, sharing, singing and dancing with this playfully interactive, get-ready-for-school friend! Kasey teaches kids more than 40 school-ready skills in three key developmental areas – Academic, Social and Physical. Realistic speech, electronic display screen, interactive lights and moving head, waist, arms, hands and eyes bring Kasey to life! Games and activities make learning fun; high fives and other amazing moves reinforce learning success. Approx. 7"H. Requires 3 "D" batteries.
Ages 3 – 7 years
F3-P77899 . . . $45.00

Expand the Learning!

Kasey Software
Additional software cartridges clip right on Kasey's back to expand the fun and learning. Each sold separately and subject to availability.
Ages 3 – 7 years
$18.00 each

Math
Numbers & Counting
F3-P77955

Addition & More
F3-P77232

Science
Living Things
F3-P77954

Wonderful World™
F3-P77229

Languages
Spanish
F3-P77228

French
F3-P77953

Reading
Words & Sentences
F3-PB1363

Focus on Phonics™
F3-PB0688

267

1999–2014

To order, call 1-800-747-8697

OPPOSITE AND ABOVE: Toby the Totbot and Kasey the Kinderbot, two talking robot toys from the Fisher-Price Catalog, 2004.

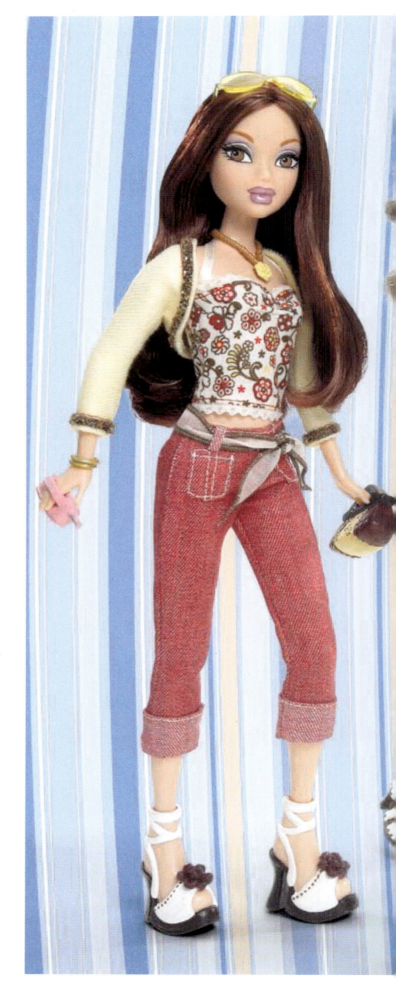

My Scene Fashion dolls, from the Mattel Girls' Toys Catalog, Fall 2005.

Lets kids SEE & HEAR themselves on TV!

A. Star Station™ Entertainment System

Your little ones can be the star of their own TV show! Kid-friendly controls make it easy for kids to run the show all by themselves: they just plug the Star Station™ base unit into your TV, pop in a music cartridge and get ready to sing along to favorite KIDZ BOP® songs—parent-approved, kid-cool versions of today's most popular hits sung by kids for kids.™ They can play, pause, and select songs with just the push of a button. They can choose and change special effects lenses through the wireless microphone. They can even plug it into any CD/MP3 player to sing along to other favorite songs! They'll think it's cool to see and hear themselves on TV, and as you watch them perform, you'll see their self-esteem and self-confidence grow. System connects easily to a TV or VCR to record each special performance. TV must have Audio/Video input jacks. Microphone requires 3 "AAA" batteries; base unit requires 6 "C" batteries.

Ages 3 years & up   F3-H6723 . . . . . $60.00

Includes base unit, wireless microphone and one music cartridge with these hit KIDZ BOP® songs:

1. All Star
2. Hey Ya
3. Doggy (Who Let The Dogs Out)
4. SK8ER BOI

TV not included.

Featuring hit music from

KIDZ BOP

Today's most popular songs sung by kids for kids™

Fisher-Price

B. Star Station™ On-the-Go Player™

In the car, at the store, wherever you go—kids can carry their tunes! They just pop in a Kidz Bop® music cartridge and they're ready to rock...and roll! Kid-friendly controls for play/pause/skip, kid-sized headphones, and durable music cartridges make it easy for them to operate all by themselves. Flexible clip lets them attach it anywhere for hands-free portability. Works with any Star Station music cartridge. Requires 3 "AAA" batteries.

Ages 3 years & up
F3-H8908 . . . . . $20.00

Includes one music cartridge with these hit KIDZ BOP® songs:

1. Trouble
2. Beautiful Soul
3. Can't Fight The Moonlight

C. Star Station™ On-the-Go Microphone™ NEW!

Real working microphone lets little entertainers perform on-the-go! They just pop in a Kidz Bop® music cartridge and sing along. Kid-friendly controls for volume and play/pause/skip and durable music cartridges make it easy for them to operate all by themselves. Wireless mic is easy-to-grip, even for the smallest hands, and it won't limit their dance moves! Works with any Star Station music cartridge. Requires 3 "AAA" batteries.

Ages 3 years & up
F3-J0222 . . . . . $15.00

Includes one music cartridge with these hit KIDZ BOP® songs:

1. I Like It
2. Absolutely (Story Of A Girl)
3. Purple People Eater

More Star Station/ KIDZ BOP® music cartridges online at www.fisher-pricestore.com

The Star Station musical toy range, from the Fisher-Price Catalog, 2006.

D. Shake 'n Go Speedway™

Shake the racers to start their engines, then let 'em go on the Speedway! You'll hear lots of real-time, play-by-play phrases from an announcer as the cars race around the track. That's because this "smart" speedway actually knows who's winning—and it announces the champion at the end of each race! Lights and real racing sound effects add to the fun and excitement. Includes two Shake 'n Go™ Racers. More Shake 'n Go Racers, each with its own unique engine sound, sold separately. Speedway requires 4 "AA" batteries; each racer requires 3 "AA" batteries.
Ages 3 years & up
F3-H4088 . . . . . $40.00*

*Gift wrapping not available.

BEST TOY AWARD PLATINUM — OPPENHEIM TOY PORTFOLIO

Rrrrrr!

"Red 5 is in the lead!"

VRRROOOM!

E. Hot Rod
F3-G5780

F. Rally Car™
F3-G5779

G. Exotic Car™
F3-G5788

H. Police Car NEW!
F3-J3987

I. Race Car
F3-G7734

Shake 'n Go™ Racers

These cool cars are shaking things up with a whole new way to race! Just shake a car to start its engine; each one has a different sound. The more you shake them, the further they go! Race them up to 20 feet (6 m), or race them on the Shake 'n Go Speedway™ (sold separately above). Each Racer sold separately. Requires 3 "AA" batteries.
Ages 3 years & up
$8.00 each

K. Prototype Racer™ NEW!
F3-J3986

J. Stock Car
F3-G5787

To order, call 1-800-747-8697

Fisher-Price

35

The Shake 'N' Go Racers and Speedway Set, from the Fisher-Price Catalog, 2006.

Barney & Friends was created in 1988 in Dallas, Texas by Sheryl Leach, a mother and former teacher who noticed a need in the market for song-based children's videos. Leach's *Barney & the Backyard Gang* videos sold well regionally, eventually gaining a national audience thanks to Connecticut Public Television executive Larry Rifkin, who was impressed by a Barney VHS he rented for his daughter. He pitched the idea of a Barney television series, and *Barney & Friends* debuted to acclaim on PBS in 1992, the start of a 22-year run that would cement the big, purple dinosaur as a pop culture phenomenon.

Toymakers, publishers, and clothing companies were all eager to license the beloved dinosaur in the early 1990s, and soon Barney merchandise was available in almost every possible category, followed by live-based experiences and entertainment. In 1996, Barney kicked off a sixty-city tour seen by almost two million fans, and released his first feature film in 1998.

Barney arrived at Mattel with the 2012 acquisition of HiT entertainment, and continues to be in the zeitgeist; in addition to talk show and comedy skit mentions, DVDs, books, and toys including plush dinosaurs and play figure sets, a new animated series, *Barney's World*, premiered on Max in October 2024 to great excitement.

OPPOSITE AND ABOVE: Barney toys and accessories, from the Fisher-Price Catalog, 2006.

Barney™

94416 **Toot 'n Squirt Sub**™   **NEW!**
- Sub makes bubbles when immersed in water
- Periscope squirts water
- Press BJ™ down for fun tooting sound
- Removable Barney™ can be placed in submarine or used for free-play activity
- All pieces float
- Ages over 18 months

94576 **Peek-A-Boo House**   **NEW!**
- Ring the bell & open the door to find one of 3 friends!
- Take-along toy that features character phrases & melodies
- Includes 2 "AA" (R6) batteries
- Ages over 12 months

Toot Toot

Ding! Dong!

Ding! Dong!

94793 **Bathtime Pals Assortment (3)**
- A bathtime buddy for fun in the tub
- Made of soft terry cloth
- Convenient loop for easy drying
- Machine washable & dryer safe
- Available in Barney™, BJ™ and Baby Bop™
- Collect all 3
- Ages 12 months & up

94795 Barney™

94796 Baby Bop™

94797 BJ™

Fun in and out of the tub!

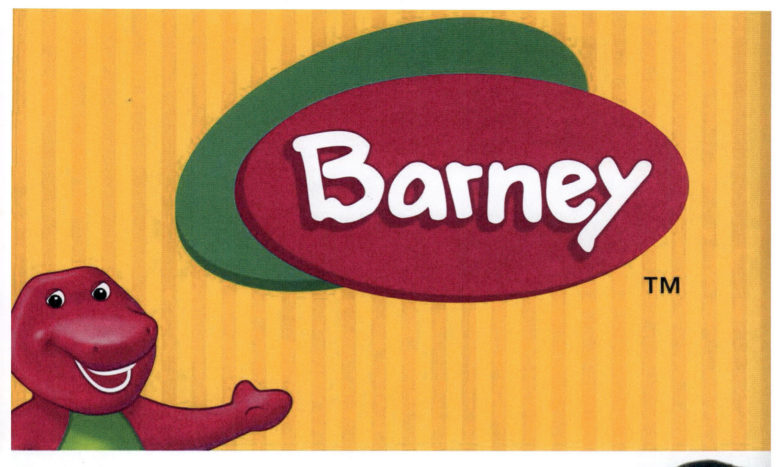

94686 Flash 'n Sounds Funlight™   **NEW!**

- Blast off to outer space with Barney™!
- A real-working flashlight with space sounds, a fun tune & Barney phrases!
- Light flashes as the music plays
- Includes 3 "AA" (R6) batteries
- Ages over 12 months

"3-2-1 Blastoff!"

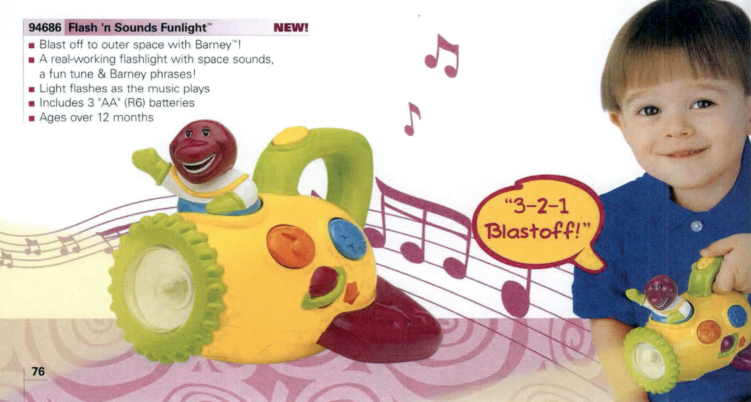

76

OPPOSITE AND ABOVE: Barney toy line assortment, from the Fisher-Price catalog, Fall 2001.
FOLLOWING PAGES: The 2007 Hot Wheels Monster Jam line, from the Mattel Catalog, Spring 2008.

BARBIE® *B* COLLECTOR

**Barbie® Fashion Model Collection
Violette™ Barbie® Doll
Platinum Label™**

The first breath of spring demands a gala celebration! Perfect for entertaining or being entertained, Violette™ Barbie® doll joins the Barbie® Fashion Model Collection dressed for a stylish ball. She wears a gown made of printed silk organza over a satin underdress and tulle petticoat with lilac taffeta trim. It's a springtime vision of the ultimate romantic, retro ball gown – finished with violets in her hair! Doll cannot stand alone or hold purse as shown. Ages 14 and over.

J4254 STD. PAK 1
UPC CODE: 27084-32059-6

Barbie® Fashion Model Collection
Highland Fling™ Barbie® Doll
Gold Label™
Barbie® Fashion Model Collection launches its own British
invasion – beginning with Highland Fling™ Barbie® doll.
Perfect for sleeping or relaxing, the terrific tartan nightwear
pays tribute to the United Kingdom. Bold hues and girly
Gaelic touches create a sweet ensemble, that's perfect for
a spot of tea – en suite! Doll cannot stand alone. Doll stand
included. Cart and tea set not included. Ages 14 and over.
J0939 STD. PAK 4
UPC CODE: 27084-29323-4

OPPOSITE: The Violette doll in the Fashion Model Collection, from the Mattel Girls' Toys Catalog, 2002.
ABOVE: The Highland Fling doll in the Fashion Model Collection, from the Mattel Girls' Toys Catalog, Spring 2006.

**HOT WHEELS® MONSTER JAM®
REV TREDZ™ Assortment**

Kids can't wait to rev these 1:43 scale monster trucks up and let 'em loose to climb right over obstacles! With a powerful friction motor and ferocious wheel action, these monsters are just like the big guys on the Monster Jam® circuit. Each truck features an authentic, highly-detailed deco of one of your favorite monster trucks. Each sold separately, subject to availability. Colors and decorations may vary. Open box. Ages 3 and over.

89853 ASST. PAK 12
UPC CODE: 26676-89853-6

© 2007 Mattel, Inc. All Rights Reserved. © 2007 Live.

HOT WHEELS® 1:64 MONSTER JAM® Assortment
Bring home the action of the Monster Jam® circuit with these authentic 1:64 scale monster trucks! Complete with die-cast chassis and bodies, highly-detailed decos, oversized tires and chrome-like rims, these trucks look just like the actual trucks form the world's largest monster truck circuit. The 2007 assortment continues the Undercoverz™ (tilt-body) sub-segment, while adding new Shoxx™ vehicles that feature working suspension. Each sold separately, subject to availability. Colors and decorations may vary. Not for use with Hot Wheels® sets. Blister card. Ages 3 and over.
21572 STD. PAK 12
UPC CODE: 74299-21572-8

© 2007 Mattel, Inc. All Rights Reserved.

© 2007 Live Nation Motor Sports, Inc. United States Hot Rod Association®, Monster Jam®, and Blacksmith®, Blue Thunder®, Bulldozer®, El Toro Loco®, Grave Digger®, Junkyard Dog™, Maximum Destruction®, Monster Mutt™, Power Forward™, Radical Rescue™, Ragin' Steel™, and Sergeant Smash™ are trademarks of Live Nation Motor Sports, Inc." © 2006 SFX Motor Sports, Inc., a Live Nation company.

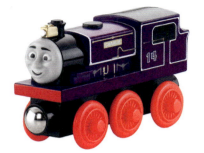

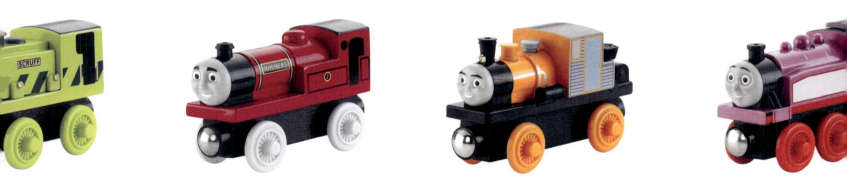

The Railway Series of children's books, written by Christopher Awdry—that were inspired by his father, the Rev. Wilbert Awdry's, stories from his youth—was adapted into the television show *Thomas & Friends* in 1984 by Britt Allcroft, a writer and producer. Allcroft and her crew used live action models operated by radio controls with static figures of humans and animals. The charming characters and wholesome plotlines appealed to parents and kids, and the show was an immediate hit in the United Kingdom. A spin-off called *Shining Time Station* was created to repackage *Thomas & Friends* for the American market, which ran on PBS Kids from 1989–1996.

In 2002, HiT Entertainment purchased Allcroft's production company, transitioning *Thomas & Friends* to full CGI animation by 2009, allowing for more action and expression from characters and giving each his or her own unique voice.

In 2012, Mattel purchased HiT and welcomed *Thomas & Friends* to the Mattel family with an accompanying toy line including wooden rail sets and train cars (metal die-cast for older fans, plastic for littler ones.) *Thomas & Friends* continued to add more diverse characters and even a new theme song. Finally, in 2020, *Thomas & Friends* completed its run, making way for a brand new 2-D animated television show called *Thomas & Friends: All Engines Go*, in 2021.

OPPOSITE AND ABOVE: The Thomas & Friends line.
FOLLOWING PAGES: The Imaginext line, from the Fisher-Price Catalog, 2013.

Imaginext® Pirate Ship New!

Ahoy, mateys! Imagine sailing under the Jolly Roger flag, as Captain of your very own pirate ship! Turn figures on disks to raise the anchor, lower the sails, and pop out the plank. Twist the dial to stage a sword duel; push buttons to reveal the row cannon, and fire! Shiver me timbers—it's a new pirate adventure every time you play! Includes 2 crew, 2 swords, row cannon, 3 cannon balls, and repositionable Jolly Roger flag. Not intended for use in water. Approx 19"L x 18½"H.

3–8 yrs / $55 / F3-W9596 /

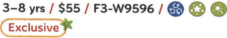

 Exclusive

282

1999–2014

Add more swashbuckling excitement!

Imaginext® Pirate Whale New!

Blimey! Watch out for mouth-chomping action and moving fins! Press the launcher to "spout" a water blob. Not intended for use in water.

3–8 yrs / $14 / F3-X7660

   / **Exclusive**

Skeleton Pirate Captain & Officer New!
3–8 yrs / $7 / F3-X7645
Exclusive

Skeleton Deckhands New!
3–8 yrs / $7 / F3-X7646
Exclusive

Pirate Captain & Officer New!
3–8 yrs / $7 / F3-X7647
Exclusive

Pirate Deckhand & Cannon New!
3–8 yrs / $7 / F3-Y9365
Exclusive

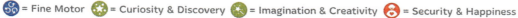

= Fine Motor = Curiosity & Discovery = Imagination & Creativity = Security & Happiness

"Man the bridge!"

"Protect the castle!"

 imaginext.

Unfolds to over 3 feet long!

B-Boom!

Eagle Talon Castle with ActionTech™

Actually recognizes and responds to Imaginext® ActionTech™ accessories with exciting voice phrases and battle sound effects! Turn figures on disks to activate the castle defenses: talons lock the gate, shutters barricade the windows and the mighty eagle's head is revealed. Launch disks out its mouth! Comes with 32 play pieces, including ActionTech cannon. Approx. 42"L x 16"H. Requires 2 AA batteries.
3–8 yrs / $50 / F3-W9635 /

Knight & Eagle
3–8 yrs / $8 / F3-W9548

Castle Knight & Horse New!
3–8 yrs / $8 / F3-X7633

Roaarr!

Dragon
with ActionTech™
Lunge and snap action! Bring it to your Eagle Talon Castle to unlock even more special sounds and phrases. Approx. 11"H. Requires 2 AA batteries.
3–8 yrs / $35 / F3-W9554

Royal Coach New!
with ActionTech™
Turn figure on disk to arm the coach for battle mode, then FIRE! Bring it to your Eagle Talon Castle to unlock even more special sounds and phrases. Requires 2 AAA batteries.
3–8 yrs / $15 / F3-X7635

Find Imaginext® Dinosaurs online, too!

fisher-pricestore.com / 1-800-747-8697

"Here, toys have **always** been art."

CHAPTER SIX

Play is for Everyone

Over the past decade, Mattel has taken great strides to fulfill the Handlers' original mission: to create beautiful, functional toys at affordable prices for every child, and to act with purpose and intention in committing to new initiatives to support that overarching ethos.

American Girl has expanded and diversified in big ways thanks to technology that makes on-demand customized toys possible. In 2019 Mattel launched the Creatable World program, which allows girls to create a truly custom doll with a wide variety of skin tones; face shapes and smile options; hair colors, textures, and styles; eye colors; and other customizations like freckles, glasses, pierced ears, braces, and hearing aids.

2015–2025

American Girl also added accessories to provide more representation, including an allergy and asthma kit, wheelchair, service dog vests, a diabetes care kit, and crutches. These options made it possible for so many more girls to see themselves represented by their dolls.

Barbie is the most inclusive and diverse doll line in the world, with the strong and consistent objective of inspiring every girl to believe that they can be and do anything. In 2016, Mattel introduced three new body types for Barbie: curvy, petite, and tall, with a cover and feature article in Time magazine. The goal was to have Barbie reflect a wider range of girls, so that every girl could find a Barbie that felt authentic to her. That same year, Barbie ran for President again (having run for President in almost every election cycle since 1992) as part of the first all-female ticket. The play pack came with President Barbie and Vice President Barbie, available in a variety of skin and hair color options.

But Barbie's reach achieved never-before-seen heights with *The Barbie Movie*, directed by Greta Gerwig and starring Margot Robbie as Barbie, which made cinematic history in 2023. It broke multiple box office records, including highest-grossing film of the year, and the soundtrack album was nominated for eleven Grammy awards. The film's theme of female empowerment, authenticity, and dealing with societal pressures and gender norms resonated with women of all ages who saw themselves reflected in Barbie's journey to self-acceptance. The film quickly became a cultural phenomenon and led to a sharp increase in sales of Barbie and the rise of Barbie-core fashion and décor looks, proving that Barbie, who has always represented choices for girls from fashion to careers to lifestyle, was just as relevant and inspiring now as she had been back in 1959. Barbie has continued to be at the forefront of storytelling for a new generation of girls, via a multi-pronged content approach that includes YouTube, social, gaming, a Netflix animated series, and publishing initiatives.

Barbie wasn't the only Mattel brand going big. Hot Wheels debuted a new show on Netflix, *Hot Wheels: Let's Race!*, featuring kid racers and their vehicles that help them overcome different challenges. They also launched the annual Hot Wheels Legends Tour—the global search for the next Hot Wheels that invites car builders to enter their custom builds for a chance to be immortalized as a Hot Wheels die-cast. The tour has become a global phenomenon, with millions of fans of all ages around the world.

Truly, the spirit of inclusion and community has been embraced holistically by most every division of Mattel. In 2017 UNO came out with a special deck for color-blind kids, following that in 2019 with a braille deck. Now color-blind versions of games including Phase10, Blokus, Skip-Bo, and Ker Plunk are all available. In 2022, Thomas & Friends introduced a new autistic character, Bruno the Brake Car, showing that diversity and representation can be a part of shows even without human characters.

Mattel has also doubled down on its commitment to research ways to make toy production more sustainable and environmentally friendly. Mattel's PlayBack program launched in 2021 and allows consumers to return old toys so they can be recycled into new Mattel products. In 2022, Barbie created a Jane Goodall Barbie and a line of Eco-Leadership Team dolls, all Certified Carbon Neutral dolls made from recycled ocean-bound plastic. The Eco-Leadership Team dolls show Barbie in four careers that protect the planet and promote sustainability, including Chief Sustainability Officer, Conservation Scientist, Renewable Energy Engineer, and an Environmental Advocate.

The belief and vision that a kinder, more inclusive, and equitable future can be nurtured and built through childhood play is what has always set Mattel apart from the competition, and that principle is what will keep Mattel growing and innovating into a bright future.

2015–2025

OPPOSITE, CLOCKWISE FROM UPPER LEFT: Covers from the Mattel catalogs from Spring 2015, Fall 2021, Fall 2017, Spring 2019, and Fall 2022.

Catalog Archive

Zomby Gaga, the Lady Gaga Monster High doll, introduced in the Mattel Catalog, Spring 2016.

ABOVE AND OPPOSITE: Zomby Gaga and the Monster High Core Collection, from the Mattel Catalog, Spring 2016.

The Barbie Fashionistas lineup, collected in the Mattel Catalog, Fall 2016.

Hot Wheels Stunt garage, from the Mattel Catalog, Spring 2017.

ABOVE: The Matchbox 75 collection, from the Mattel Catalog, 2020.
FOLLOWING PAGES: Blokus, from the Mattel Catalog, Fall 2017.

ABOVE AND OPPOSITE: Barbie Careers dolls, from the Mattel Catalog, Fall 2016.

ABOVE: Enchantimals, from the Mattel Catalog, Fall 2017.
OPPOSITE: My Mini MixieQ's, from the Mattel Catalog, Fall 2017.

PREVIOUS PAGES: Masters of the Universe figures, from the Mattel Catalog, Fall 2021.
ABOVE: Polly Pocket Compact Playsets, from the Mattel Catalog, Fall 2023.

The Polly Pocket Monster High Compact Playset, from the Mattel Catalog, Fall 2023.

Faboolous Friends Monster High Doll Collection, from the Mattel Catalog, Fall 2022.

Hot Wheels City track sets, from the Mattel Catalog, Fall 2018.

Hot Wheels Monster Trucks, from the Mattel Catalog, 2018.

313

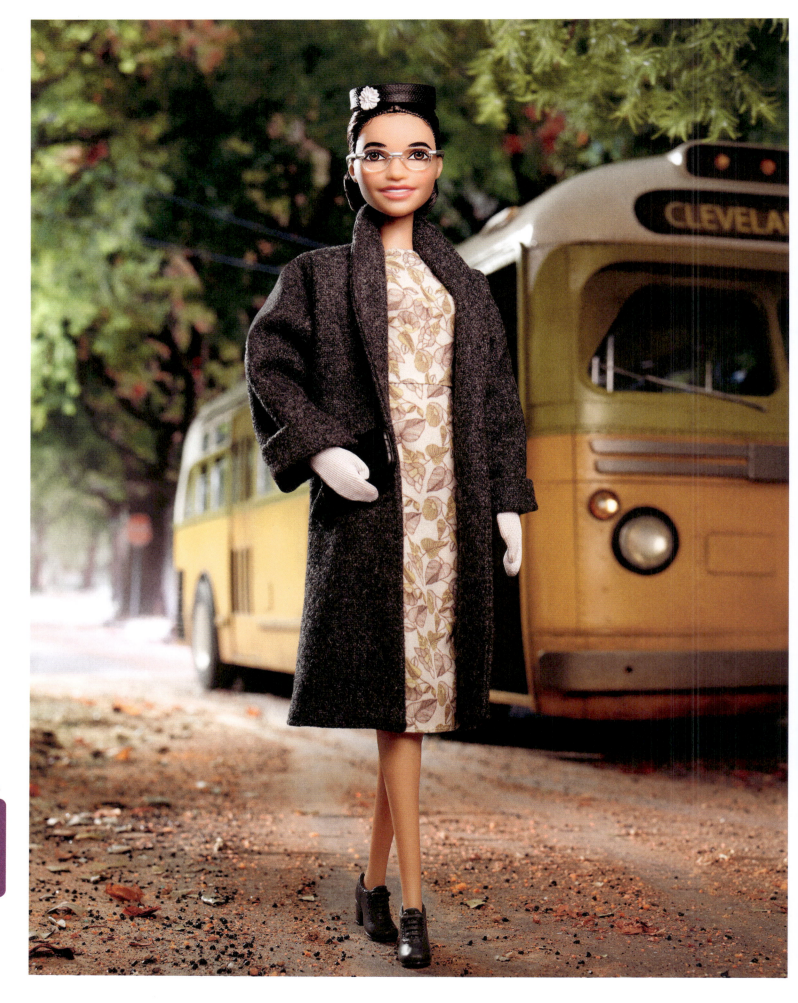

ABOVE AND OPPOSITE: Dolls from the Barbie Inspiring Women series, from the Mattel Catalog, Fall 2018.

Barbie. SIGNATURE
Celia Cruz
SINGER, PERFORMER
"QUEEN OF SALSA"
INSPIRING WOMEN™ SERIES

Barbie. SIGNATURE
Wilma Mankiller
PRINCIPAL CHIEF OF THE CHEROKEE
NATION OF OKLAHOMA
INSPIRING WOMEN™ SERIES

Barbie. SIGNATURE
Amelia Earhart™
AVIATOR
INSPIRING WOMEN™ SERIES

Barbie. SIGNATURE
Anna May Wong
ACTRESS
INSPIRING WOMEN™ SERIES

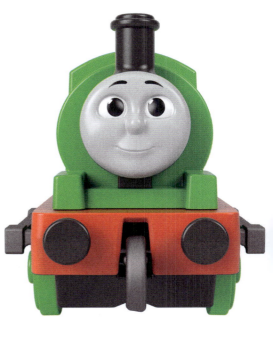

ABOVE AND OPPOSITE: Thomas the Tank Engine and Friends, from the Mattel Catalog, Spring 2019.
FOLLOWING PAGES: Little People core collection, from the Fisher-Price Catalog, 2021.

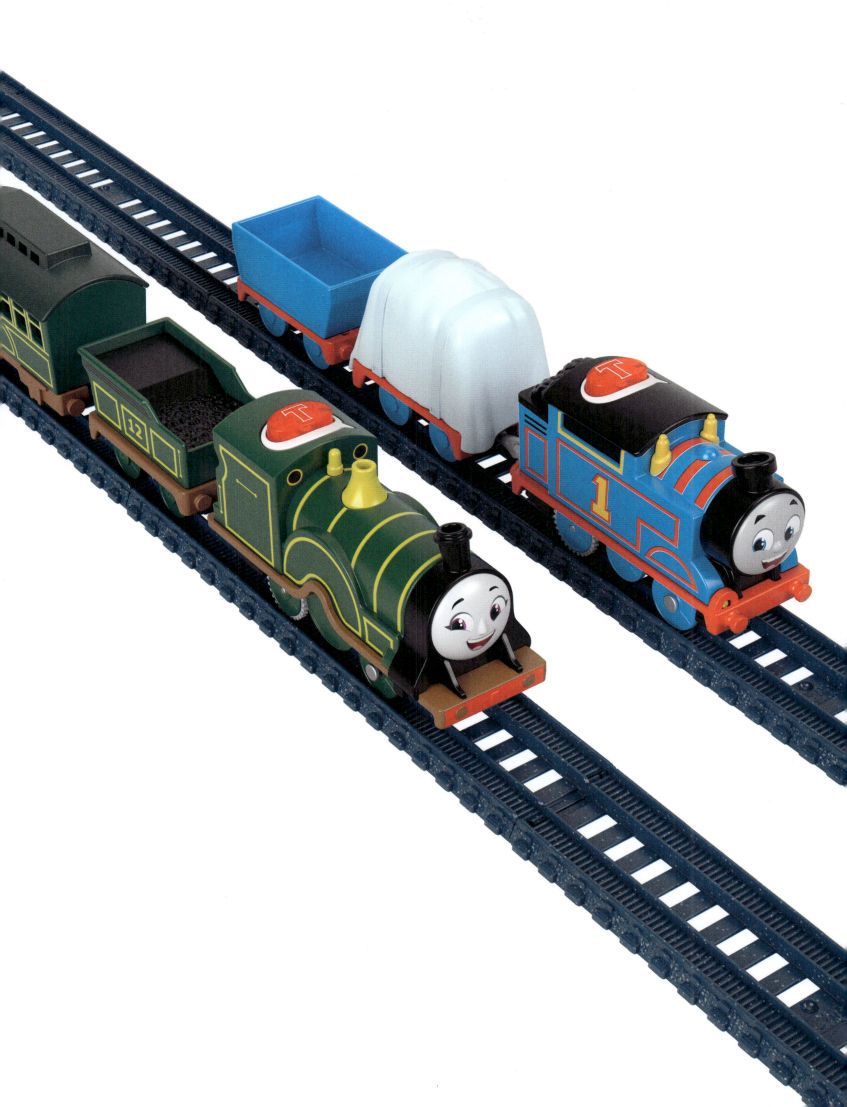

Courtney™ 1986

Valley girl vibes

In the '80s, California girls like Courtney just wanted to have fun...at the mall, of course! The raddest place was the arcade, where one quarter could make any gamer a high scorer.

All the '80s essentials in one ultimate collection.

Courtney™ 18" Doll, Book & Accessories $146 *You save $5*

Courtney™ 18" Doll & Book Only GRN41 $115

Courtney's™ Accessories Only GRN42 $36
©2020 Lip Smacker is a trademark of Markwins Beauty Products, Inc. All rights are reserved.

Courtney's™ Totally Tubular Collection HCL59 $284

You Tube
▶ YouTube Kids

Waka waka waka! Watch Courtney change the game with your family on YouTube, or have your girl watch on YouTube Kids.

26   AMERICANGIRL.COM | 800-845-0005 | AGES 8+

320

2015–2025

The introduction of Courtney, from the American Girl Catalog, 2022.

twinning = winning

MARCH 2023

New! HISTORICAL CHARACTERS

meet Isabel AND NICKI

1999

American Girl

ABOVE: The introduction of Isabel and Nicki, from the American Girl Catalog, 2023.
FOLLOWING PAGES: The Truly Me collection, from the American Girl Catalog, 2023.

truly me ✧

Find a FRIEND for life

Introducing new dolls and **outfits** that encourage girls to express who they truly are.

American Girl
Styled by You
EXPERIENCE

More style is in store! Scan to discover a new experience for your girl.

NEW! Truly Me™ 18" Doll & Book $125
American Girl® Doll Carrier for Girls / HRN83 $36

New!

#100
#122
#126
#124
#113
#132
#118
#127
#115
#114
#103
#117
#112
#110
#108
#107
#116
#130
#104
#101
#100

Complete her look with a mini backpack & accessories or a mini Coconut Chip™ pup!

NEW! **AG™** Star Squad Puppy & Accessories / JFB48 $32
NEW! **AG™** Star Squad Mini Backpack & Accessories / JFB49 $32

See all doll choices at americangirl.com/truly-me.

PREVIOUS PAGES: *Barbie the Movie* pink Corvette convertible, from the Mattel Catalog, Summer 2023.
ABOVE: *Barbie the Movie* Collectible Doll, Margot Robbie as Barbie in Pink Power Jumpsuit, from the Mattel Catalog, Summer 2023.

Barbie Signature Ken Doll wearing "I Am Kenough" Hoodie. *Barbie the Movie*, from Mattel Creations, Summer 2023.

Barbie the Movie Collectible Dolls Inline Skating Outfit, from the Mattel Catalog, Summer 2023.

Barbie the Movie Collectible Ken Doll wearing Denim Matching Set, from the Mattel Catalog, Summer 2023.

Barbie the Movie Weird Barbie Doll, from Mattel Creations, Summer 2023.

Barbie the Movie Collectible Doll President in Pink and Gold Dress, from the Mattel Catalog, Summer 2023.

Barbie the Movie Fashion Pack plus Collectible Doll Pink Western Outfit, from the Mattel Catalog, Summer 2023.

Barbie the Movie Collectible Doll Gold and White Disco Tracksuit and Gold Disco Jumpsuit, from the Mattel Catalog, Summer 2023.

Barbie the Movie MEGA Dreamhouse, from the Mattel Catalog, Summer 2023

331

UNO: Barbie the Movie, from the Mattel Catalog, Summer 2023.

ABOVE: UNO Fandom MOTU Game, from Mattel Creations, Spring 2024.
OPPOSITE: UNO Fandom Monster High Fearbook Deck, from Mattel Creations, Spring 2024.

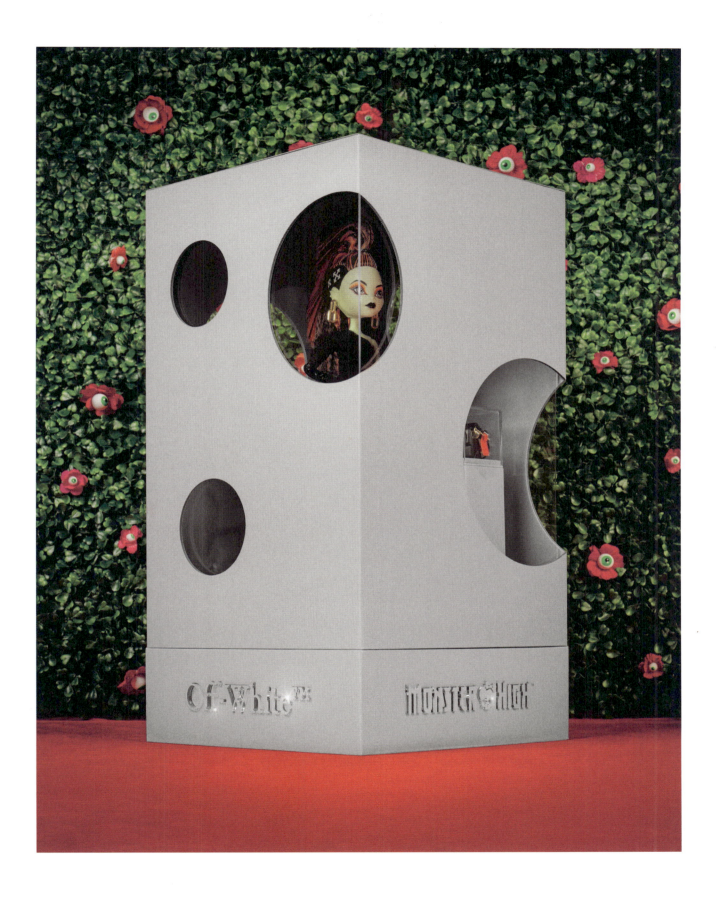

Off-White™ c/o Monster High Doll Collection, from Mattel Creations, Fall 2023.

ABOVE: Fisher-Price Barney's World Lights & Sounds Treehouse Playset With Figures For Preschool Kids, from the Mattel Catalog, Spring 2025.
OPPOSITE: Fisher-Price Barney's World 8-inch plush Barney Toy Dinosaur, from the Mattel Catalog, Spring 2025.

Masters of the Universe Origins Castle Grayskull Playset with figurines, from Mattel Creations, Fall 2022.

ABOVE: Barbie Signature, 2022 Convention Exclusive A Date with Destiny Barbie, Summer 2022.
OPPOSITE: Barbie Signature, 2022 Convention Exclusive Chromatic Couture Green Barbie, Spring 2022.
FOLLOWING PAGE: Barbie Signature 65th Anniversary Doll, inspired by the 1959 iconic black-and-white striped swimsuit, Spring 2024.

Where **Play** *Happens*

First published in the United States of America in 2025 by
RIZZOLI INTERNATIONAL PUBLICATIONS, INC.
49 West 27th Street
New York, NY 10001
www.rizzoliusa.com

Copyright © 2025 Mattel.
MATTEL™ and associated trademarks are owned by Mattel.

Publisher: Charles Miers
Editor: Jacob Lehman
Production Manager: Kaija Markoe

For Mattel:
Creative lead: Lizz Wasserman
Project editor: Elana Cohen
Archivists: Eliana Ruiz, Melissa Huntington

Designed by CMYKayleigh
Typeset in Editorial New by Pangram Pangram and Roc Grotesk by Kostić Type

All rights reserved. No part of this publication may be reproduced, stored in a
retrieval system, or transmitted in any form or by any means, electronic, mechanical,
photocopying, recording, or otherwise, without prior consent of the publishers.

2025 2026 2027 2028 / 10 9 8 7 6 5 4 3 2 1

ISBN: 978-0-8478-7589-4
Library of Congress Control Number: 2025933351
Printed in Italy

The authorized representative in the EU for product safety and compliance is
Mondadori Libri S.p.A., via Gian Battista Vico 42, Milan, Italy, 20123
www.mondadori.it

MIX
Paper | Supporting
responsible forestry
FSC® C084761
FSC
www.fsc.org